JANE AUSTEN,
EDWARD KNIGHT,
&
CHAWTON

Commerce & Community

JANE AUSTEN, EDWARD KNIGHT, & CHAWTON

◆

Commerce & Community

Linda Slothouber

Woodpigeon
Publishing

Jane Austen, Edward Knight, & Chawton
Commerce and Community
By Linda Slothouber

Printed in the United States of America

♦First printing, 2015♦

ISBN 978-0-692-31974-1

Woodpigeon Publishing
305 Swarthmore Avenue
Gaithersburg, MD 20877
woodpigeonpublishing.com

Contents

Image Credits

Other photographs and graphics by the author.

Acknowledgments

In February 1813, an American turned up in Chawton. Unwell and presumably without money or local connections, the American stayed in Chawton for five weeks, supported by a small weekly allowance from the parish. This charity was documented in the account book of the Overseers of the Poor, but the name of the American went unrecorded, and there is no indication whether this visitor took to the road again or came to rest in the churchyard.

A more fortunate American in many ways, I arrived in Chawton in July 2013. My six-week stay there, without which I could not have written this book, was supported by a grant from the Jane Austen Society of North America's International Visitor Program. I thank JASNA, the IVP Committee, and JASNA's New York Region, which founded this excellent program. The Old Stables at Chawton House Library was my temporary home, and I am very grateful to the entire Chawton House Library staff for their warm welcome, as well as for the matchless opportunity to explore the land, buildings, and books that once belonged to Edward Knight. Thanks also to the many kind individuals associated with Jane Austen's House Museum, the Jane Austen Society of the UK, and Chawton House Library who gave me tips on research resources and extended their hospitality to me through family dinners, garden parties, excursions, and invitations to join in their meetings and activities.

I thank the staff of the Hampshire Record Office, who provided access to documents in their care as well as indispensable research support after I returned home. Thanks also to Rebecca Lilley of the Godmersham Heritage Trust, who conducted research and compiled documentation from the Trust's archives, and to Maria Sienkiewicz, Barclays Group Archivist, who provided photographs of Edward Knight's bank records.

Many more people made this book possible, and I am grateful to them all. Deirdre Le Faye and Jane Hurst shared their own research with me and responded to many, many questions over more than a year. Tom Carpenter, Ann Channon, Sarah Parry, Christine Grover, Maggie Lane, Ian Rotherham, Kelly Macdonald, Ronald Dunning, Tony Corley, Steve Lawrence, Jacqui Grainger, Sheryl Craig, and Fiona Melhuish contributed important pieces of the puzzle in their respective areas of expertise. Jane Hurst, Deirdre Le Faye, Maureen Stiller, Richard Knight, Sue and Martyn Dell, Jeremy and Carol Knight, Sarah Parry, Twila Glenn, and Carol Wright very kindly read an early draft of this book. Its present form owes much to their comments and insights, but any errors are mine alone.

My thanks to editor Debra Roush for her sharp-eyed review and sensible counsel, and to Susan Van Epps, Amy Patterson, and Maureen Stiller, who advised me on marketing. Family members, friends, and JASNA colleagues who encouraged me to apply for the International Visitor Program and cheered me on over the past year know who they are, and I thank them all. Finally, I must acknowledge with gratitude and love Chris Amigo, Mr. Woodpigeon himself, who with interest, intelligence, and humor has played a part in every stage of this project.

George Knightley converses with his brother, John...

As a magistrate, he had generally some point of law to consult John about, or, at least, some curious anecdote to give; and as a farmer, as keeping in hand the home-farm at Donwell, he had to tell what every field was to bear next year, and to give all such local information as could not fail of being interesting to a brother whose home it had equally been the longest part of his life, and whose attachments were strong. The plan of a drain, the change of a fence, the felling of a tree, and the destination of every acre for wheat, turnips, or spring corn, was entered into with as much equality of interest by John, as his cooler manners rendered possible...

–Jane Austen, *Emma*

Sketch, circa 1809, of a street in Chawton.

Introduction

In a letter to her sister-in-law in 1820, Cassandra Austen[1] wrote about the concerns and achievements of her surviving sons. Describing her third son, Edward, the owner of several large estates, Mrs. Austen said, "He has a most active mind, a clear head, & a sound Judgment; he is quite a Man of Business..." No doubt some landed gentlemen, those with the self-regard of Jane Austen's character Sir Walter Elliot, would have objected to being labeled a "man of business," but the fact is estate ownership *was* a business, and one worthy of the attention of a responsible landowner. In Jane Austen's novels, we glimpse Mr. Darcy writing his letters of business from Netherfield and Mr. Knightley meeting every week with his bailiff; we see Fanny Price's attitude toward Henry Crawford change when he begins to show a proper interest in the people and activities on his estate.

The details of estate ownership that we see in the novels are, for the most part, probably not modeled on specific situations and events. The reader of *Emma* cannot help but be intrigued by a brief note in the Chawton estate accounts for February 1813 recording the forced removal of "gipsies" who had set up camp in Chawton Park, and perhaps some such interesting occurrences found their way into the pages of her books, but for the most part, she had little need to conduct research. Her work is grounded in her lifelong familiarity with the structure and rhythms of English country life.

From her youth in Steventon, Jane Austen knew estate-owners, such as the Harwoods at Deane House, as well as tenants of large properties, such as the Bigg-Wither family of Manydown Park and the Digweeds at Steventon Manor. Later, Jane's visits to her brother Edward's home and her eight-year residence in the village of Chawton gave her additional insight into a landowner's concerns and relationships with tenants, tradespeople, laborers, and the functionaries of government and the church. From 1813, Edward Knight resided for short periods at Chawton House (known then as the Great House) or lent it to his brothers, and many visits were made back and forth between

---

[1] *Cassandra Austen, née Leigh (1739-1827) and George Austen (1731-1805) were the parents of James, George, Edward, Henry-Thomas, Cassandra-Elizabeth, Francis-William, Jane, and Charles-John Austen. Jane and James were deceased by the time Mrs. Austen wrote her letter.*

the Great House and the cottage in the village where Mrs. Austen, Jane, Cassandra, and their friend Martha Lloyd lived. It is surely no coincidence that *Emma*, composed in 1814 and the early months of 1815, shows an acute understanding of a landowner's activities and responsibilities.

About This Book

My aim in beginning this book was twofold: to provide a historical context for Jane Austen's allusions to estate management in her novels, and to help those who study or visit the village of Chawton understand the estate economy there. Along the way, I learned quite a bit about Edward Knight—his character and relationships, as well as his business activities. Other portraits began to develop, too, of the people who participated in the estate economy in and around Chawton. As these individuals came into clearer view and took their places in my mental picture of Chawton in the early 19th century, I gained a better understanding of Jane Austen's eight years among them.

The history of Chawton and the world portrayed in Austen's novels suggest many fascinating topics which have been already addressed by experts, whose work I will not attempt to duplicate here. The tourist wanting to learn the history of specific buildings and compare the Chawton of today to the village that Jane Austen would have known can consult *Jane Austen and Chawton*, *Jane Austen and Alton*, and other publications by historian Jane Hurst. Those seeking details about events in the lives of Jane Austen and her family will find Deirdre Le Faye's *Chronology of Jane Austen and Her Family*; *Jane Austen: A Family Record*; and *Jane Austen's Letters* invaluable. Le Faye's most recent book, *Jane Austen's Country Life*, provides a comprehensive picture of rural life and work. I have drawn from all of these sources, as well as records in the Hampshire Record Office and The National Archives; the customer ledgers of Goslings Bank; newspapers; the *Reports* of the Jane Austen Society of the UK; and *Persuasions*, the journal of the Jane Austen Society of North America.

Limitations in Primary Source Materials

Much of the information in this book is derived from records belonging to the Knight family and held at the Hampshire Record Office. Financial records, land records, maps, and estate-related correspondence survive, some dating back to the 16th century, but this body of documents is understandably incomplete. Many items that would be interesting to a modern researcher were never saved, and some documents suffered damage over time. Few estate records survive from 1794 to 1808, and those that do are mostly damaged beyond use; estate accounts from 1820-1832 are missing as well. Edward Knight's account records at Goslings Bank, acquired and preserved by Barclays Bank, help to some extent to fill the gap.

Fortuitously, one of the best-documented periods in the history of the Chawton estate (1808-1819) encompasses the years that Jane Austen lived in Chawton and finalized or composed her novels (1809-1817). I have focused principally on this period, with excursions into the decades before and after when a broader perspective is desirable.

Notes on Names

Edward Austen and his family changed their surname from Austen to Knight in 1812. For consistency, I refer to them by the Knight surname throughout the text. Elizabeth Austen, Edward's wife, died before the change of surname; "Elizabeth Knight" herein refers not to her, but to the early-18th-century heiress to the Knight estates, Elizabeth (née Martin) Knight. When writing of Edward (Austen) Knight and his son, also named Edward, I use the convention "Edward Knight I" and "Edward Knight II" for clarity. The same convention is observed for Thomas Knight and his identically named son.

The frequency with which certain surnames occur can be confusing, and the reader is cautioned not to assume that there is a family connection unless it is stated. For example, Robert Trimmer, a wealthy lawyer, may or may not have shared a remote ancestor with William Trimmer, laborer; the same goes for the land-owning Knights and the poorer Knights who populated many Hampshire villages. If a distant kinship existed, none of them seems to have known of it. To my knowledge, the only instance where Jane Austen alluded to a (spurious) relationship between Edward Knight and a villager was a humorous one: in 1798, she described a bit of deception by Mr. and Mrs. Austen, who, in trying to help a Steventon villager named Knight secure the lease of an ale-house, allowed its owner to believe that he had an opportunity to "oblige a relation of Edward."

For compound names, I have followed the 19th-century British convention of linking the equivalent elements with a hyphen. Thus, John-Rawstorne Papillon possessed two given names, for example, while James-Edward Austen-Leigh had both two given names and a compound surname.

Notes on Money

Pounds, shillings, and pence are expressed in this book as they were written in the source records. Thus £2.10.6 is two pounds, ten shillings, and sixpence; £0.2.0 is two shillings. There were 12 pennies to a shilling and 20 shillings to a pound. A guinea was a small gold coin equivalent to £1.1.0. For some transactions, such as contributions to charity, prizes, and some salaries, a sum was often provided in guineas rather than pounds as a matter of custom. I have deliberately not provided modern equivalents for sums of money that appear in old records. Such comparisons are problematic, and it is more informative for the purposes of this work to compare different values within the time period—for example, incomes of different individuals, or costs for particular commodities or services.

References and Bibliography

Because this book is intended for general readership yet relies on many documentary sources, I have elected not to include reference citations within the text. References and a bibliography appear at the back of the book.

Essential Terminology

COUNTY: Administrative division of the nation, originally based on the Anglo-Saxon shire. In the early 19th century, the leading government officials at the county level were the Lord Lieutenant, 20 Deputy Lieutenants, and the Sheriff. Magistrates and justices of the peace administered the law. Steventon and Chawton were in the County of Southampton, informally known as Hampshire.

PARISH: Unit of ecclesiastical and civil government with legally defined boundaries and one church. Each parish had a rector, who held a living (i.e., a house, the authority to collect tithes, and the duty to ensure services were performed in the church) but did not necessarily reside in the parish. The parish vestry was equivalent to a local council. Tax collection, road maintenance, and other civil matters were handled at the parish level.

VILLAGE: Settlement of houses and shops, larger than a hamlet and smaller than a town, in proximity to a church. The term has no standard definition, and the boundaries of a particular village were a matter of common understanding rather than law. Many landowners owned large parts of the villages adjacent to their seats, and a few owned entire villages.

MANOR: Lands put under the control of an individual by a superior and then distributed to others as part of the feudal system. Also refers to the rights that the Lord of the Manor enjoyed or could assign to others, including advowson (the right of presenting a clergyman of his choice to a parish) and "the liberty of a manor" (freedom to shoot game). Manorial tenants were obliged to pay fees to the Lord of the Manor. The steward was the Lord of the Manor's official representative at manorial court meetings.

ESTATE: Collectively, the land and assets passed by inheritance from one individual to another ("a man of such good estate as Mr. Crawford"). Also used to refer to property held in one area ("all the Pemberley estates") or a gentleman's seat ("the estate at Delaford"). The steward or agent of an estate provided practical management of business matters; the estate steward and the manorial steward were often, but not always, the same person.

SEAT: The house and property considered a gentleman's home ("Principal seat, Kellynch Hall").

LANDS-IN-HAND: Land not rented to tenants, but retained for the landowner's own pleasure or money-making efforts using his own workforce.

RECTORY: A house, with associated lands, occupied by a rector (i.e., a clergyman in charge of a parish) or his appointee. Alternately, the clerical office of rector ("the valuable rectory of this parish"). An estate owner typically owned the advowson, but the church owned and administered the property used by the rector, who was supported by the tithes of the parish. A vicar performed the same duties as a rector but did not receive the full tithes.

GLEBE: Church-owned land used by a rector or vicar to supplement his income. Glebe land could be farmed or rented out.

Edward Knight at the time of his European Grand Tour.

1. Edward Knight

Edward, third son of George and Cassandra Austen, was born on October 7, 1767, at their home, the parsonage of Deane in Hampshire. As a young child, he was small; his mother observed that he was comparable in size to his brother Henry, who was nearly four years his junior. Henry, writing in 1848, recalled Edward's appealing "personal beauty" as a child. If young Edward was more delicate, perhaps less boisterous than his brothers, his gentle manner may have had the greatest consequences for his future.

Edward Knight as a boy.

In 1779, Thomas Knight II, a distant relation of the Austens, and his new wife Catherine visited the Austen family at Steventon rectory as part of their honeymoon journey. Charmed by 12-year-old Edward, they took him along for the rest of the trip. Later, they invited the boy for other holidays and long visits to their home at Godmersham Park in Kent. Thomas Knight II was the son of the man who had appointed George Austen to be the rector of Steventon in 1761, and now a second mark of favor was bestowed on the Austens. When he was about fifteen, Edward was adopted by Thomas and Catherine Knight, who had no children of their own, and thereafter was educated and groomed to inherit their substantial wealth. He made a four-year Grand Tour, visiting Italy, Switzerland, and Germany. He spent time at the royal court of Saxony and is believed to have attended the university in Dresden for a year (although, according to Mrs. Austen, "classical knowledge and literary taste" were not among his gifts).

In 1791, Edward married Elizabeth Bridges, from a prominent Kent family, and they began life together at Rolling Place (now called Rowling), a small former manor house owned by the Bridges. In 1794, Edward's adoptive father Thomas Knight II died. Although Edward was the acknowledged heir, Knight left the use of his property to his wife for her lifetime.

"I continued my walk ... to a large heap of snow, being curious to make a snowball in August. I paid [for] my curiosity by getting perfectly wet in the feet and then went contented back and found the dinner already served, which consisted of a miserable soup partly of stewed goat and partly of marmote, an animal they find in these mountains, in its make resembles a cat, in color a monkey. I saw it before it was skinned, and was by no means prejudiced in its favor. At dinner however we all eat of it heartily ... "

*Edward Knight's Journal,
August 13, 1786, Oberwald, Switzerland*

Four years later, Catherine Knight decided not to make Edward wait longer, and she initiated legal proceedings to transfer control of the Knight estates entirely to him, reserving an allowance of £2,000 a year for herself. When Catherine Knight died in 1812, Edward and his children formally adopted the Knight surname.

Edward's own heir, also named Edward, was born in 1794 (a year later than daughter Fanny, who as a female could not inherit under the terms of the entail[2] controlling the Knight estate). Nine more children followed. Shortly after the birth of the last, in 1808, Elizabeth died suddenly. Edward never remarried. He relied on his daughter Fanny, then only fifteen, to take on much of the work of running the household and bringing up the younger children.

Edward held many public roles in Kent, where his principal home, Godmersham Park, was located. In 1792, he became a Deputy Lieutenant for the county, a post that during wartime involved organizing the selection of men to serve in the militia. In 1794, he enlisted as a cornet[3] in the Wingham Yeomanry (based near his home in Rowling) and was promoted the following year to lieutenant. In 1803, when the threat of invasion from France was acute, he organized the Godmersham & Molash Company of the East Kent Volunteers and was its captain. He served for several decades as a magistrate, adjudicating on matters large and small and participating in county government. He accepted the prestigious, largely ceremonial one-year post of High Sheriff of Kent in 1801, but never sought a seat in Parliament. His name often appeared in newspapers among the organizers or supporters of charitable and civic endeavors: he was the treasurer for the Kent & Canterbury Hospital,

[2] Entail: a legal mechanism controlling the inheritance of an estate, usually over several generations. Some—but not all—entails restricted inheritance to males only. Others limited inheritance to heirs "of the body," excluding adopted children.
[3] Cornet: a military rank equivalent to a second lieutenant.

a patron of agricultural and laborers' benefit societies, and a contributor to charitable collections raising money for poor widows, debtors, and those distressed by famine in Ireland.

A Portrait Drawn by Many Pens

Family letters and narratives preserve various descriptions of Edward's character and habits. Anna Lefroy (James Austen's elder daughter) described Edward's disposition as "so sweet and yielding, his whole character so opposed to contention of every kind that he never could have been, under any circumstances, an irritable or discontented man." Several family members mentioned his kindness and ability to amuse children. Even after his wife's death, he made Godmersham a happy home: Edward's sister Cassandra worried that "so much happiness in their youth[,] ... so indulgent a father and so liberal a style of living" might not prepare his children for the challenges of adult life, but he did take steps to give them a practical education and to pass on his country-squire values. For example, he gave his daughter Fanny her own cow when she was only six so that she could watch it being cared for and, in due time, receive the money from selling its calf. During visits to Chawton, Edward and his young son toured the estate on horseback so that the future heir could get to know the property that would one day be his.

Edward was diligent in his duties as a landowner. Caroline Austen (James's younger daughter) wrote that "he must have been more his own 'man of business' than is usual with people of large property, for I think it always was his greatest interest to attend to his estates." His distinctive spiky handwriting on documents in the Knight Archive reveals the "man of business" at work: here and there are his detailed annotations on maps, his calculations of acreage and money, his signature on accounts. In the public sphere, he participated in agricultural societies and took positions on issues based on how they would affect his and his tenants' farms—for example, he opposed canals and railways and supported the opening of a new corn market. His practical turn of mind and his eye for agriculture are evident in his only recorded comment on his sister's novel *Emma*: he is said to have teased Jane about depicting apple trees in blossom at the same time that the strawberries were ripe at Donwell Abbey.

Jane Austen wrote, "I know no one more deserving of happiness without alloy than Edward is." He bore major challenges—such as his massive losses from his brother's business failure and the scandal of his son's elopement—with equanimity, but he suffered occasional bouts of anxiety and malaise and sometimes felt himself to be seriously ill. There are clues (not least of which is the fact that he lived to the age of 85) that the source of these distresses was more mental than physical. When one of their naval brothers adopted a daring new hairstyle, Jane hoped that Edward would not hear of it, "lest it might fall on his spirits and retard his recovery." On a dreary day many years later, she declared, "Edward's spirits will be wanting sunshine." She expressed sympathy, but little apparent worry, when reporting on his "Bowel complaints, Faintnesses & Sicknesses" on one occasion and a "little feverish indisposition" on another. At Bath, Jane thought that "the bustle of sending for Tea, Coffee, & Sugar, &c., & going out to taste a cheese" might do him more good than the electricity treatments he was determined to try.

Stained-glass window at Chawton House showing the coat-of-arms of Edward Knight.

Edward had the wealth to enjoy the social life of London, but he was not much attracted to it. When Jane wrote of attending a glittering party where guests filled the house and famous musicians entertained, it was her brother Henry, not Edward, who was the host. Edward was in London when peace was declared in the war with France, yet again it was Henry, not Edward, who went to the grand ball attended by the King and Prince Regent. When Edward visited the metropolis, it was for business or for his family's benefit. Jane wrote about accompanying him and his daughters on errands to shops and to the dentist, with a family visit to the theatre as an evening treat. On at least one occasion, he escorted his nieces, either Frank's or Charles's daughters, around the city; under his wing, "the Misses Austin" [sic] rated a mention in the London Standard's report on fashionable arrivals. He took four of his children to Paris for two weeks in 1817, but otherwise his Grand Tour seems to have sated Edward's appetite for ambitious travel. When it was time for his own sons to see something of the continent, Edward II and George took a year-long tour on their own, and Henry Austen was deputed to accompany the younger boys to France and Switzerland.

Despite Edward's affability toward family and his disdain for cutting a fine figure in society, he had a tough side as well. Once he assumed control of the Knight property, he was determined that no one was going to cheat him out of any bit of it. When a tenant absconded without paying rent, or someone cut trees on his land, he strongly asserted his rights and moved quickly to collect money to which he was entitled. His reach extended beyond farmers: he felt it within his rights to remind a noble debtor, the Marquess of Hastings, of his "sacred obligation" to pay Edward's "just demands." Edward kept bank clerks on their toes, correcting mistakes in their ledgers. Long after his son reached adulthood and established himself at Chawton, the elder Edward still traveled regularly from Godmersham to Chawton to meet with his steward and go over the Hampshire accounts in detail.

Family Ties

It seems inevitable that Edward's adoption by the Knights and the elevated style of life that became his would have created some distance between him and his birth family. In 1799, Jane wrote to her sister Cassandra, "I am tolerably glad to hear that Edward's income is so good a one—as glad as I can [be] at anybody's being rich besides You & me"; in later years, she could not help but observe how "the Elegance & Ease & Luxury" of Edward's home contrasted with the "Vulgar Economy" under which she, her mother, and sister lived. In an 1820 letter to her sister-in-law, Mrs. Austen wrote of her sons James, Henry, Frank, and Charles by their given names, but referred to her third son, though with no less affection, as "Mr. Knight."

Edward was unapologetic about his good fortune, which should be no surprise—legions of English eldest sons who inherited estates while their siblings had to find their own way in the world seldom bothered to reflect on the fairness of the system. Nonetheless, he maintained strong relationships with the Austens by supporting their endeavors and by involving them in his activities and concerns.

The trustees and witnesses of Edward's marriage settlement were all Kentish connections of Thomas Knight or the Bridges family except for one: Edward's eldest brother, James Austen. Jane's letters provide glimpses of Edward designing a hen-house with his mother, comparing notes on pigs with his father, and showing his siblings around his plantations. In 1813, Edward relied on Cassandra to give him detailed reports on the status of renovations at Chawton Great House and relay instructions to his builders. The following year, when he was embroiled in a lawsuit, Edward sought Jane's help with paperwork; she, apparently quite happily, deferred her travel plans to remain on hand to take down any "memorandums" he might dictate.

> "My brother ... desires me to say that your being at Chawton when he is will be quite necessary. You cannot think it more indispensable than he does."
>
> *Jane Austen relaying messages from Edward to Cassandra by letter, October 11-12, 1813*

The Austen women played an important part in the lives of Edward's children, particularly after his wife Elizabeth's death.

In 1824, when "a gradual but decided failure of bodily strength" convinced him that he was about to die, Edward wrote a letter of advice to his son and heir. His most strongly expressed wish was that his son would be "a second Father as well as an affectionate Brother and Friend" to his siblings. Edward had taken on a similar role after the death of his own father in 1805. In addition to eventually providing a home for his mother and sisters, he lent Chawton Great House at various times to his naval brothers and extended his hospitality at Godmersham to his siblings and their guests. He paid for the care of his disabled brother George for many years, and he provided significant financial support for Henry's career as a banker and army agent. He created annuities for his siblings to help them manage their savings, and he paid his lawyers to handle legal business for the family.

A "Prosperous and Placid Life"

Edward Knight's companion in his last years was his daughter Marianne, who never married. On November 19, 1852, after a carriage ride around Godmersham the previous evening, Edward Knight died in his sleep, closing what one relative termed a "prosperous and placid life." His obituary in the *Kentish Gazette* suggests his habits and temperament had remained steady throughout his long life:

> We have now lost almost the last of that school of country gentlemen of which England has been so proud, and they will hereafter exist only in memory and books.... Mr. Knight, though nearly the last, was a worthy specimen of this generation. Until prevented by the infirmities of age, he yearly visited his estate in Hampshire, and spent the remainder of his time, in the bosom of his family, at Godmersham Park, where he superintended his own affairs almost to the last. The deceased was no bigot in religion or politics—moderate in all his views, he took no leading part in the political challenges of the day, but was quiet and unobtrusive.... He was for many years a most useful and active magistrate, possessing a calm and well reputed mind, he gave a patient hearing to everyone... Mr. Knight was also a useful adviser in public and parochial business.

In his will, Knight directed that he should be buried at either Godmersham or Chawton, whichever was closer to his place of death. He was attended to the church of St. Lawrence the Martyr in Godmersham by family and "a long list of tenantry desirous of paying their last tribute of respect to so good a landlord" and was interred in the Knight family vault.

2. The Knight Inheritance

Thomas Knight II adopted Edward Knight as his heir, but we must look back one generation further, to Thomas Knight I, to understand the extent of the land that Edward inherited and the long process by which it became his. Thomas Knight I, born Thomas Brodnax, was the first to possess both the Hampshire and Kent properties that later came to Edward, and it was he who made it possible for Edward to eventually inherit them. It is through his marriage that Austens came to be connected to Knights, and through his beneficence that George Austen became rector of Steventon. Although

Thomas Knight I and the Acquisition of His Estates

	Thomas Brodnax	
Born to William Brodnax and Anne May (1701)		1726: Inherits Godmersham from father, some Sussex property from mother
Heir to Sir Thomas May (mother's cousin)	changes surname to May	1727: Inherits May property in Sussex and London 1729: Marries Jane Monk, granddaughter of Jane Austen of Kent
Heir to Elizabeth Martin Knight (second cousin)	changes surname to Knight	1738: Inherits Knight properties in Hampshire 1755: Breaks Elizabeth Knight's entail 1781: Dies, leaves estate to son, Thomas Knight II

Thomas Knight I had no idea that his son would be childless and look to his Austen relations for an heir, he broke an entail that would have prevented Edward Knight from inheriting the Knight estates.

The Kent Properties

The Brodnax family had lived for several generations in Godmersham, near the town of Ashford. Their house, called Ford Place due to its proximity to a ford in the River Stour, was an Elizabethan mansion, and they owned most of the land in Godmersham parish. When Thomas Brodnax (later Thomas Knight I) inherited the estate, he replaced the old house with a fashionable Palladian house. He improved the gardens, enclosed the park, and changed the name of the estate to Godmersham Park. By the time Edward Knight inherited it from Thomas Knight II, the mansion house and surrounding woods, pastures, and fields encompassed 1,330 acres. Additional land, roughly 900 acres in Godmersham and surrounding parishes, was leased to tenants to produce rental income.

Thomas Knight I, his son Thomas, and Edward Knight in turn made Godmersham Park an ideal gentleman's seat, catering for the pleasures of its inhabitants and guests. A large herd of deer grazed the parkland. Kennels, a lodge, and a game larder served the needs of sportsmen. Three summerhouses and a boathouse provided more relaxed recreation. Natural scenery could be enjoyed on walks, such as the Serpentine Walk and River Walk. Edward Knight improved the views from the mansion and its grounds by relocating village houses from in front of the house, rebuilding them outside the park.

Godmersham Park as pictured in Neale's *Views of the Seats of Noblemen and Gentlemen,* 1824.

The Hampshire Properties

In 1774, Thomas Knight I, perhaps looking toward the day when his son would inherit his estates, directed his steward to draw up a list of all his Hampshire properties. Although some sales and purchases were made during the next two decades, the 1774 list is broadly representative of the Hampshire land that Edward Knight inherited in his turn. It showed that, in a county that measured just about one million acres, Thomas Knight I owned roughly 6,800 acres, distributed through 34 parishes. Most of this property was concentrated around the market town of Alton and the nearby village of Chawton, reaching east to Neatham, south to Colemore, west to Bentworth, and north to Shalden. (Knight did not own everything within this area, but he was the principal landowner.) Knight also owned almost the entire parish of Steventon and land in nine adjacent parishes, as well as a large farm in Winchester.

Thomas Knight II, who adopted Edward Austen as his heir to the Knight estates.

The Elizabethan manor house of Chawton, along with the surrounding farms and woodlands, was the jewel of the Hampshire properties. Chawton was one of 55 manors in Hampshire that William the Conqueror had granted to Hugh de Port in the 11th century. King Henry III and his successors in the 13th and early 14th centuries traveled along the royal road to Chawton, hunted deer in Chawton Park Wood, and stayed at the medieval manor house (of which no traces remain aboveground). In 1524, Hugh de Port's descendants leased Chawton to William Knight. William's son John Knight purchased it in 1551 and acquired the rights of the manor and advowson (which could be sold separately from the tangible property) in 1578. His son, another John, constructed much of the current Great House in the late 16th century.

The direct line of the Knights ended in 1679 with the death of Sir Richard Knight, and the estate passed to the grandchildren of his paternal aunt, Dorothy Martin. Three Martin children, Richard, Christopher, and Elizabeth, held the estate in succession, all taking the Knight name, but none of them had children of their own. Elizabeth Knight passed Chawton and the other Knight properties in Hampshire to her second cousin, Thomas Brodnax May—who became Thomas Knight I. Thus, the Knights' Hampshire lands were added to the properties Thomas had received from his father and those he inherited from Sir Thomas May.

Elizabeth (Martin) Knight, who left the Knight property in Hampshire to Thomas Knight I.

15

Thomas Knight I physically transformed the estates in his possession. At Steventon, he bought out five farmers so that he owned most of the property in the parish, then rearranged the farmlands and rented them with strict new convenants. He added to his holdings in the vicinity of Alton by acquiring property in Neatham and Colemore. At Chawton, he pushed successfully for the enclosure of the common lands. Acts of enclosure, passed by Parliament on a parish-by-parish basis, formally transferred ownership of the common fields to local landowners, with those who already owned the most receiving the largest shares of the common land. Enclosure led to the consolidation of property and the displacement of the small farmers who could not meet their share of the costs for surveys and legal work and could not afford to enclose their land, while the poor lost their traditional rights to pasture animals and gather wood on the common. The 1741 enclosure at Chawton divided the common land among just nine parties, with allocations ranging from 11 acres, granted to one Michael Harris, to 286 acres, granted to Thomas Knight I.

By the time Edward Knight came into his inheritance more than fifty years later, the Hampshire estates were for the most part stable and peaceful. The effects of enclosure had been absorbed. Many long-term tenants were in place, such as the Digweeds in Steventon and the Andrews family in Chawton, who had settled on their respective farms in the 1750s. No controversies or major changes were in view, and most of the residents at Chawton could not remember a time when a Knight had lived full-time at the Great House.

Painting of Chawton Great House by Mellichamp, circa 1740. The buildings of Manor Farm are at far left, the Old Stables near left, and the Church of St. Nicholas at right.

Other Properties

Over several generations, the Brodnaxes, Mays, and Knights had acquired, by marriage, legacy, or purchase, many pieces of land scattered throughout southern England. The Knight estate changed over time as land was added and land was sold. Property that left Knight ownership before Edward Knight's time included the Martins' family estate at Eynsham, Oxfordshire; much of the Sussex property that Thomas Knight I had acquired from Sir Thomas May; and property in Devon.

When Edward Knight assumed ownership of the Knight estate in 1798, it included property in Sussex, Essex, and Middlesex (London), as well as Kent and Hampshire. In Sussex, there was a large farm on very fertile land near Southwick, which had been brought into the estate by Jane Monk. Near Chelmsford in Essex was another large farm.[4] In Middlesex, the Knight property consisted of a complex of buildings on St. Martin's Lane, London, that had been constructed at the order of Thomas Knight I (who had to obtain an Act of Parliament to do so); he named them May's Buildings to honor the man who gave him his second inheritance.

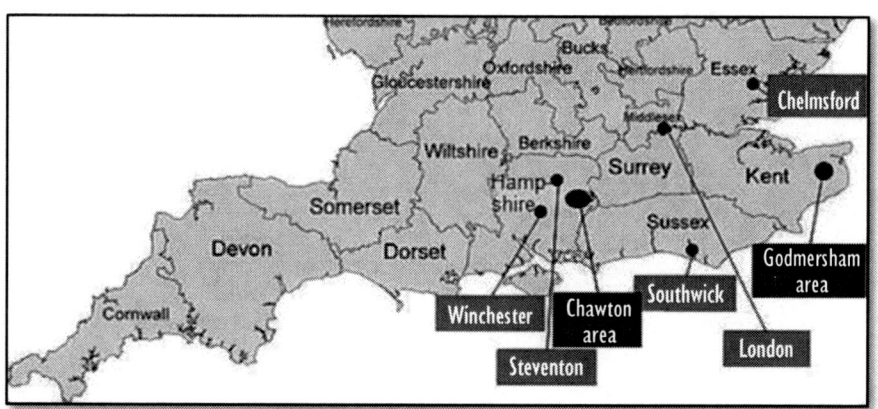

Locations of Edward Knight's property. (Dots are not to scale)

---

[4] *The location and nature of the Essex property is a matter of some speculation. An 1815 document changing the inheritance terms of the Knight estate lists the five counties cited here as locations of Knight property, but does not further identify the holdings. Goslings Bank records reveal regular payments from an Essex bank into Edward Knight's account, as discussed in the Appendix, from which I have extrapolated the Chelmsford location.*

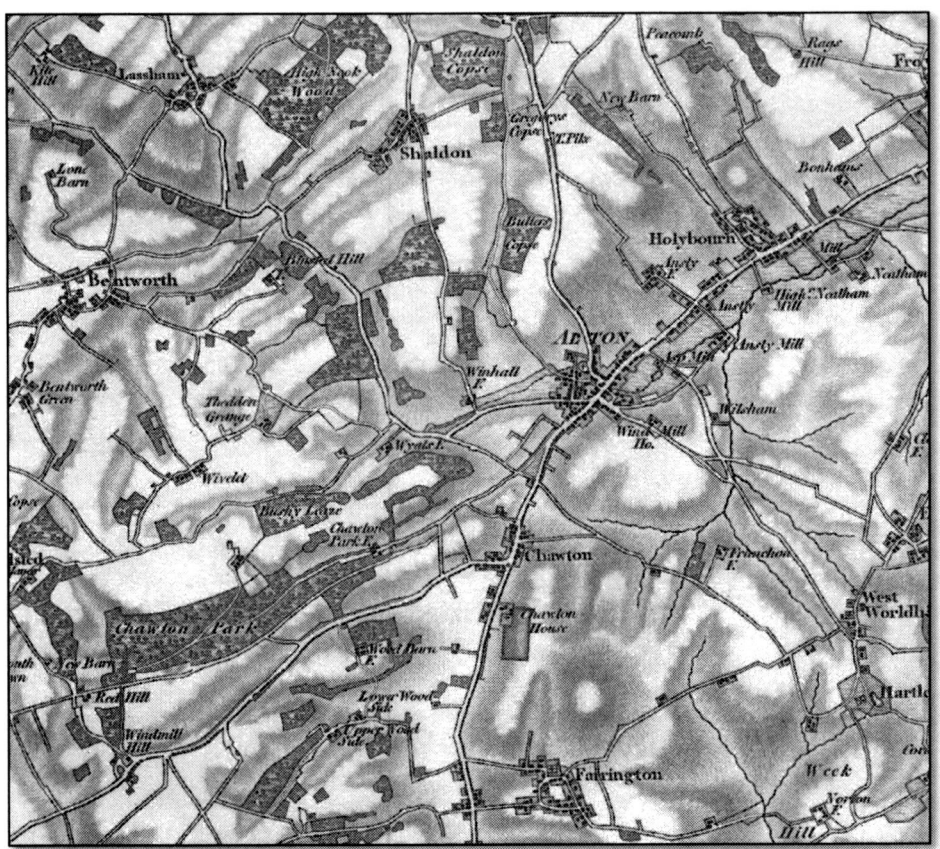

The Knight property in Hampshire was concentrated around Chawton. In this map from 1810, Alton is slightly right of center; clockwise from top are Shalden; Holybourne, Neatham, and Anstey; Truncheants (Trunchon), Worldham, and Hartley; Chawton and Farringdon; Wivelrod (Wivelet); Bentworth; and Lasham (Lassham), all locations of Knight-owned land. Other large holdings in the county, not shown here, were Abbotts Barton in Winchester, to the southwest; Steventon and adjacent parishes, to the northwest; and Colemore, to the south.

3. Financial Overview

In *Pride and Prejudice*, Mr. Darcy's income of "ten thousand a year" is a topic of general discussion very soon after his arrival in Hertfordshire. Modern readers are often surprised by the openness with which financial matters were discussed and wonder exactly what such figures represent.

Statements of a landed gentleman's annual income reflected the amount he received from renting out land. In *Mansfield Park*, Mary Crawford's exclamation about Mr. Yates—"If his rents were but equal to his rants!"—alludes to this. Rental income was generally the largest and the most consistent portion of a gentleman's income, and its stability over time was often supported by entails that restricted the sale of land belonging to the

> **"If this man had not twelve thousand a year, he would be a very stupid fellow."**
>
> Edmund Bertram commenting on Mr. Rushworth, Mansfield Park

estate. Rents were also the most prestigious element of gentleman's income, since he had to do practically no work to receive them.

The owner of an estate might have additional income from investments or from agricultural or mining activities on his lands, he might have mortgages or debts, and he would certainly have operating expenses that deducted from his gross earnings, but none of these are reflected in the simple "*x* thousand a year" estimates that were publicly discussed. Rental income was an easy, effective metric by which estates—and their owners—could be characterized and compared.

Edward Knight's Income

In the first two decades of the 19th century, Edward Knight would probably have been spoken of as having about £8,000 a year. The average yearly rental income of his Hampshire properties between 1808 and 1819 was £4,278.[5] His

---

[5] *Hampshire writer Mary Russell Mitford (born 1787) wrote—admittedly based on hearsay—that Knight's Kent estate brought him £5,000 a year and his Hampshire property nearly £10,000. This is clearly wrong, as the figure given for Hampshire is double his actual gross income from that county. Her estimate that Kent income was about half of Hampshire income seems to have been reasonably accurate, however.*

Essex, Sussex, and London properties together brought in somewhat less than £1,800 per year. The rental value of his property in Kent is difficult to ascertain, but was probably less than £2,000 per year.[6] He was wealthier than the fictional landowners to whom Jane Austen assigned a specific income, except for Mr. Darcy and Mr. Rushworth. A closer look at his Hampshire accounts shows how rental income compares to real earnings.

Hampshire Income and Its Sources

Most of Knight's Hampshire earnings came from the rental of land and from other payments related to land in use by others. Edward Knight rented out many kinds of properties: substantial houses such as Chawton Great House and the old manor house at Steventon, farms of all sizes, mills, and laborers' cottages. In addition, he collected manorial fees on land effectually belonging to others in his manors (discussed in the next chapter).

Income from land rented or held by others: rents and manorial fees

Year	1808	1809	1810	1811	1812	1813	1814	1815	1816	1817	1818	1819
£	3,575	3,640	3,930	4,346	4,889	4,909	4,507	3,722	3,729	4,483	4,439	5,165

A smaller percentage, about 16%, of income came from the sale of wood and other products harvested from the land that Edward Knight held for his own use. Because the amount of wood to be cut and sold could be increased at will (within certain limits), income from this source was more variable than rental income was; when a landowner needed money, exploiting the woodlands on his property was often a first step.

Income from sales of woodland products

Year	1808	1809	1810	1811	1812	1813	1814	1815	1816	1817	1818	1819
£	735	664	1,181	771	722	605	654	431	612	511	895	2,330

The income from the Hampshire estates was not particularly diverse, because Knight did not conduct large-scale farming operations there. In Kent, by contrast, he farmed his land and raised sheep and other livestock, in addition to working his woodlands and renting out property. Knight's Hampshire gross earnings from all sources averaged £5,237 per year for 1808 through 1819.

Expenses included payments to laborers, the wages of employees on salary,

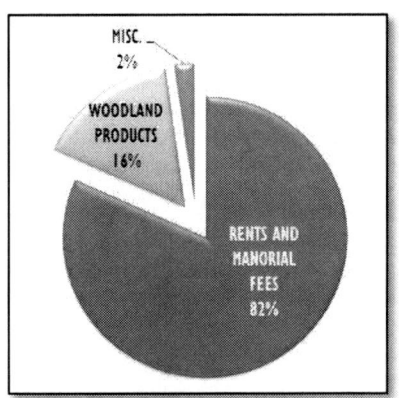

Sources of Hampshire income, 1808-1819.

---

[6] The basis for this statement and the figures that follow is detailed in the Appendix.

20

the cost of repairs to buildings and equipment, the cost of services and supplies, taxes, tithes, and miscellaneous expenses. After deduction of the expenses, the average net income (i.e., profit) of the Hampshire estates was £3,100 per year from 1808 through 1819. As a comparison, this figure is 72% of his average rental income. Knight's example shows that net income—the money that the estate-owner actually had available to spend—was significantly lower than the "x thousand a year" estimates that were commonly discussed, and which Jane Austen used as a metric of her landowning characters' wealth.

The Historical Context

The variations over time in expenses and profits align with events in Edward Knight's life and with conditions affecting the nation as a whole. Expenses were highest, amounting to more than half of gross earnings, in 1813, the year when Knight and his family spent five months at Chawton. He had to settle matters with his outgoing tenant, reimbursing him for repairs to the house and for crops he left behind. In addition, work was done to Chawton House, a donkey was hired, and a gamekeeper and dogs were brought to the estate to cater to the younger generation's sporting interests. Knight's taxes peaked in that year, adding to the total expenses.

In late 1814, Knight's ownership of his Hampshire estates was threatened by a lawsuit. James-Hinton Baverstock, an Alton brewer, contended that the breaking of Elizabeth (Martin) Knight's entail in 1755 was improperly done; as Baverstock's mother was a descendant of the Martins, he claimed ownership of the Hampshire estates on her behalf. (Nor was that the only such lawsuit: five years earlier, Edward Knight had had to contend with Catherine Heron, who laid claim to some farms that had belonged to Elizabeth Knight.) Perhaps he found it desirable then for the estates not to appear too profitable, and so the income dipped slightly for a couple of years; expenses decreased too, since there was no sense in investing more money than necessary in improvements to property he might lose.

The drop in Knight's income in 1815 and 1816 is also attributable to an agricultural crisis following the end of the Napoleonic Wars. During wartime, prices for wheat were high—bad for laborers in need of bread to feed their families, but good for farmers and those renting land to them. Once the war ended in 1815, the need to supply military forces diminished and Irish wheat began to be brought into England, depressing prices; at the same time, farmers had to pay poor rates that were driven higher when former soldiers and sailors could not find work. A law was passed in 1815 to stabilize grain prices, but its impact was delayed. Some farmers found that the cost of planting and harvesting their fields could not be recouped when they sold their crops, and many farms failed. To make matters worse, 1816 was "the year without a summer," when massive crop failures in England occurred due to atmospheric impacts from a volcanic eruption on an island in the Indian Ocean. Throughout these and the following years, landowners saw their rental income diminish as some tenants fell behind and others abandoned their farms.

The unsettled agricultural economy led to the failure of many country banks, including, in 1815, the firm of Austen, Gray, & Vincent of Alton, in which Henry Austen was a partner. Henry's London bank, Austen, Maunde, & Tilson, also failed, and Henry was declared personally bankrupt in March 1816. He also lost his posts as an army agent and Receiver General for Oxfordshire. Knight had a significant stake in Henry's business dealings. In 1815, in an unsuccessful rescue attempt, he loaned Henry £10,000, which was only partially repaid. Knight had provided a surety bond to enable Henry to obtain the Receiver General post, and when Henry could not meet his commitments, Knight had to pay £21,000 in installments over 1816 and 1817. Demands were still being made four years later, when Knight paid £865 to the War Office on Henry's behalf. In addition, between 1808 and 1815, Knight had deposited more than £23,000 of his Hampshire estate profits (and an unknown amount from his other properties) into his account at Henry's bank. Some of that money would surely have been spent before the bank collapsed, so it is unlikely he lost the entire sum, but Knight's total losses are unknown.

A settlement in the Baverstock case was reached in 1818. The Baverstocks dropped their case in exchange for a settlement payment of £15,000. Adding to the cost were enormous legal expenses for this "arduous and important business," as his lawyer described it. Although the uncertainty over Knight's ownership of the Hampshire estates was eliminated by the settlement, his troubles were not over. Throughout the 1820s, England remained in the grip of the agricultural depression that had begun in 1814. Farmers who had invested their capital and taken on debt to obtain more land during the war with France were unable to meet their commitments, and landowners experienced increasing difficulty in finding new tenants to replace those who failed. Instability in the national currency and continually rising poor rates caused additional problems.

Various records show how Edward Knight confronted all these challenges. He seems to have taken decisive, if painful, action to put each crisis behind him as quickly as he could. In 1815, he sold a massive amount of stock—at least £20,000 worth—and another £12,700 in 1816, along with over £5,000 in exchequer bills (a type of government security).[7] He also mortgaged property in

---

[7] *Knight may have taken measures, in addition to those detailed here, for which documentation does not survive; his Goslings account ledgers begin in March 1816. The 1815 stock sale is documented in a loose page written in his hand, now in the Knight Archive.*

Farringdon and in Kent, while at the same time purchasing more acreage in Kent to strengthen his holdings there and take advantage of depressed prices.

In 1818, new measures were required to pay the Baverstock settlement and address other needs. The sale of wood from the Chawton woodlands surged, and his agent made efforts to collect late rents and find tenants for vacant properties, increasing gross earnings from Hampshire in 1819 by 41% over the previous year. In 1818, Knight sold another £5,475 in exchequer bills and obtained a cash infusion of over £22,000 from his lawyer and his Canterbury bank—probably from loans and more mortgaging of property.[8] He paid off the settlement in nine months, paying £10,000 to Jane Baverstock and £5,000 to her brother, John-Knight Hinton.

Net Worth vs. Spending Power

Edward Knight's net worth was high: in 1818, he estimated that his Kent property was worth £145,000, his Hampshire lands £140,000, and other property an additional £50,000. There is a big difference between capital assets such as land and spendable income, however, and there were large demands on Knight's income. He had significant responsibilities to meet at home: he had six sons for whom he provided, variously, military commissions, university club memberships, European tours, and allowances (his eldest son received £800 a year, the others substantially less). When four of his five daughters married, there were marriage settlements to pay.

> ## "Your competency is my wealth."
>
> *Elinor Dashwood in*
> *Sense and Sensibility*

After his father's death in 1805, Knight's mother and siblings needed his assistance as well. He took over the financial support for his brother George, who suffered from an unknown disability and lived with a blacksmith's family in Monk Sherborne. He initially gave his mother £100 a year, doubling that sum later. After Henry Austen's bank failure, Knight helped Henry with a check for £25 or £50 now and then. Payments to James and Charles Austen occurred too, though many of these seem to have been regular annuity payments on investments Knight made on their behalf.

Edward Knight did not receive the income of the Knight estates until 1798, when his adoptive mother, Catherine Knight, who owned them for her lifetime, formally stepped aside. At that time, she allowed Edward to move

---

[8] *The bank ledgers show only depositors' names and amounts paid in, with no notation of source except in the case of dividends and interest. Existing bills from Knight's London lawyers, Seymour & Squibb, show that this firm handled mortgages for him, so the large 1818 deposit from them is likely to have been mortgage proceeds.*

into Godmersham Park and receive his inheritance, but her retirement came with the stipulation that he should pay her £2,000 a year for the remainder of her life. Jane Austen confided to Cassandra a wish that this part of Mrs. Knight's decision could be more widely known among those who gossiped about Knight's good fortune, because it was not a trivial obligation. Her £2,000 stipend was paid for the next 13 years; over the years for which Knight's income was known, this stipend was equivalent to nearly 60% of the net profit of the Hampshire estates. Multiple lines of evidence—such as timber sales, expenditures on repairs, and the fact that he made several property exchanges and few purchases during his first few years in control—suggest that he had little cash to spare at this period.

Mrs. Knight died in October 1812. Edward Knight had very little time to enjoy the entirety of his inheritance without worry, because in the autumn of 1814 James-Hinton Baverstock filed his lawsuit and the numerous difficulties that would cloud the next decade began. In 1824, Knight (who feared he was dying), wrote to his son and heir, referring to "incumbrances" and "charges on the estate" and tried to impress on the younger Edward "the expediency, I may say necessity of living for some years very much within your income," yet a few lines later he wrote reassuringly, "You will always have a Sum of Money at Command, which let your Income be what it may, is a most desirable and as far as Comfort is concerned a most indispensable possession." Those few lines capture the situation of the estate-owner. Land was wealth, and could be leveraged to secure loans and ensure comfort, but doing so too much or for too long could lead to disaster.

The "incumbrances" on the estate were still present decades later. In the final year of his life, Edward Knight sought a bank loan, and his will gave his son the power to defer some of the bequests to family members until it was convenient to pay them. Edward Knight was never poor, but his large family's style of life, the scope of his business activities, and his willingness to invest aggressively to pursue long-term goals meant that he had to be prudent with his income.

4. The Business of Estate Management: A Closer Look

The owner of an English estate in the early 19th century was in an interesting position. He (or, much more rarely, she) was by definition above the cares and responsibilities of the tradesman or merchant, but nonetheless needed to exercise some degree of skill and attention to keep the money flowing in; at the very least, he needed to find a competent and honest agent. The estate-owner (or landed proprietor, in Georgian parlance) was free to do what he liked with his money, without the oversight or interference of stockholders, auditors, or government regulators; however, trustees and entails often constrained what he could do with the land—in effect, they protected the estate from its owner of the moment, in the interest of future owners. The landed proprietor enjoyed a prominent position in the community, but such prominence meant that he was expected to take a leading role in solving any problem or meeting any need. His social superiority was assumed, but his character could be judged according to the well-being of his poorest cottagers.

This chapter examines how Edward Knight, the estate-owner into whose concerns Jane Austen had the greatest insight, managed his Hampshire estates. The sources of his income, with rental income predominant, are typical of many estate-owners of the era. The degree to which he involved himself in estate business was a more individual choice. His estate accounts and other sources, though sparse in details, give insight into the degree of responsibility he felt toward his tenants, others in the community, and his own descendants. Here, the estate economy is viewed from the landowner's perspective; the roles and interests of other participants are the focus of the next chapter.

Income

Rental Income

In *Pride and Prejudice*, Charles Bingley's sisters Louisa and Caroline are eager for Charles to use the £100,000 his father left him to purchase an estate. They no doubt want him to own a grand house that they can show off to others, but more importantly, they want him to join the ranks of the landed gentry. With an estate would come rental income, free of the negative associations of wealth rooted in trade.

Rental income gave an estate-owner prestige because it gave him independence: he did not have to manage employees, run a factory, or schedule his travels and pleasures around the farming calendar. With a steward or agent in place to collect the rents, he need personally do hardly anything at all in the way of business and could devote himself to genteel pastimes. In *Persuasion*, Sir Walter Elliot seems entirely insulated from his farming tenants, while Henry Crawford in *Mansfield Park* experiences a belated and short-lived awakening to the responsibilities of the landowner. They are not the ideal, however. More laudable is Mr. Darcy, whom his housekeeper calls "the best landlord"; he "assists his tenants," all of whom "would give him a good name"—but here Austen is not very specific. It is not until *Emma* that Austen depicts both landowner and tenant fully. Robert Martin's prudent management of Abbey Mill Farm enriches his landlord, George Knightley; Knightley values his tenant's good sense and does not like to imagine doing without him. Theirs is, perhaps, an atypically close relationship of trust and service, in which Knightley provides his tenant advice about marriage and Martin carries his landlord's important papers to London.

Most of Edward Knight's rental property in Hampshire consisted of farmland, though he also rented out mills, cottages for the poor, and houses, including Chawton Great House itself. Between 1808 and 1819, he had about two dozen tenants at any one time. About half of these tenants inhabited cottages (or parts

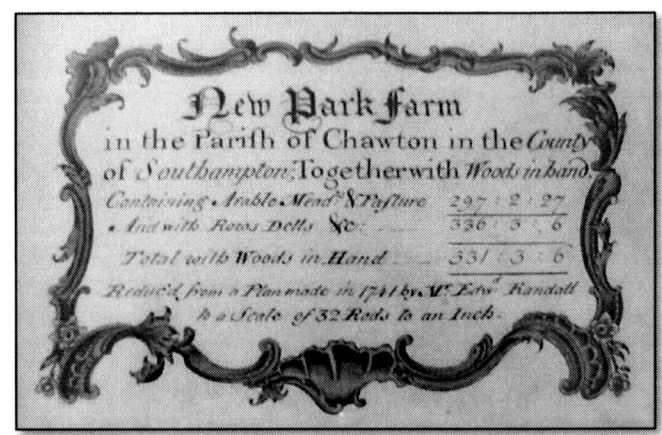

Cartouche from late 18th-century map of New Park Farm by Henry Hogben. The numbers denote land area in acres, rods, and perches. (A rod, or rood, was 1/4 of an acre, and a perch was 1/40 or a rod, 1/160 of an acre.)

of cottages) with a rental price between £1 and £10 per year; the parish Overseers of the Poor paid the rent for six of these tenements. The remaining tenants leased property at £70 per year or more, with the most expensive farm priced at more than £700. Knight raised rents on his larger properties in the early 1810s, reflecting, in part, the general rise in the value of farmland. Rents could also be changed by agreement between the landowner and tenant to reflect repairs to property, the addition or deletion of a parcel of land, and the plowing of previously unbroken pasture.

The farms worked by Knight's tenant farmers[9] were not geometrically precise blocks of land, but rather assemblages of hedged fields, irregularly shaped and identified by the same names by which owners, occupiers, and workers alike had known them for generations—names such as White Down Field, Lower Long Lands, Great Brickkiln Close, Hither 12 Acres, and Bindwood Piece (all these were at New Park Farm in Chawton). Knight kept an eye on what his tenants cultivated in their various fields. Chawton and Farringdon were on the edge of famous hop-growing country, and several farmers in the area devoted a field or two to hops, which after harvest were sent to supply breweries in London and elsewhere. Barley, which was malted for use in brewing, was also grown. Knight's tenants also grew wheat, oats, peas, and turnips, and hay crops such as sainfoin and clover. Sheep and cattle grazed in the pastures.

New Park Farm Lease Terms (1823)

14 year lease at £100 for the first year, £175 thereafter, with an increase of £20 per year per additional acre of previously unplowed pasture or meadow broken up by the tenant

Tenant will:
- Pay all rents and taxes, except as below
- Deliver yearly to Chawton House 3 loads of good wheat straw at £1.10.0 per load
- Keep everything in repair, paying half the repair bills and half the cost of nails and pins
- Properly store all corn and hay
- Not cut hedgerows without notice, nor cut hedgerows under 11 or above 13 years old
- Leave 70 acres as two years layn (i.e., sown with grass seed) at end of rental term
- Leave 65 acres as one year layn at end of rental term
- Allow the landlord to prepare for the wheat season on the above ground near end of rental term
- In the last year of the rental term, leave dung for the use of the next tenant

Landlord will:
- Supply timber, bricks, tiles, and lime (to be fetched by the tenant) for repairs; pay half the cost of nails and pins
- Pay half the repair bills (e.g., the carpenter's, thatcher's, mason's bills)
- Pay land tax
- Give the tenant room to thrash out crops, air cattle, stable four horses
- Give the tenant use of part of the house for meals, etc. (Note: The fact that Knight does not allow the tenant full use of the house indicates that the tenant is renting this as a secondary farm and does not intend to reside there.)

---

[9] *The term "tenant farmer" has carried different meanings at different times. Knight's tenant farmers rented land but were otherwise independent of their landlord; they provided their own capital and sold their produce themselves.*

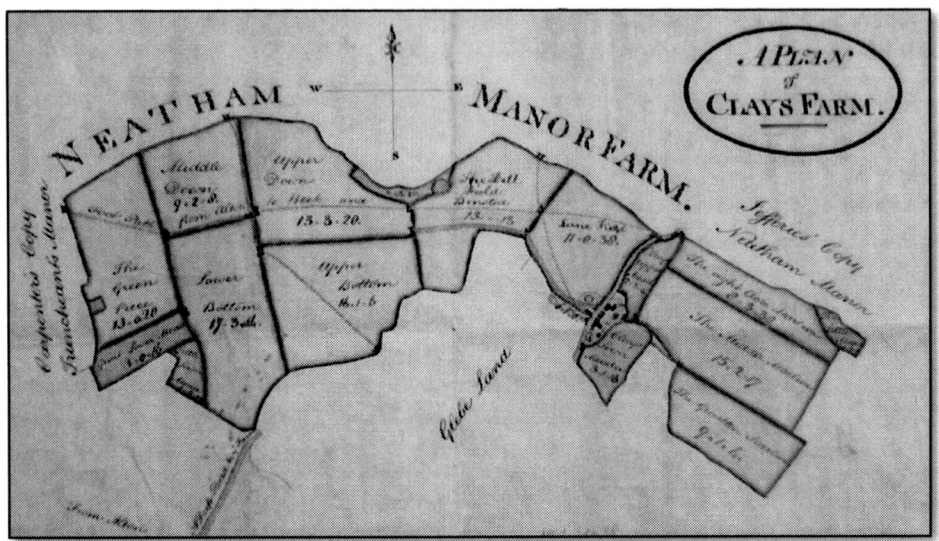

This map of fields comprising Clay's Farm in Neatham, which Edward Knight purchased in 1811, illustrates how fields were irregularly shaped, interspersed with meadows, and crossed by footpaths.

One thing that Knight's tenant farmers could not cultivate for profit was wood: Knight reserved the rights to all trees. This was a common practice, and one about which Knight was particularly adamant. Independent farmers in Chawton, such as William Baigen, sold their own wood, but Knight would not allow his tenants to become his competitors in the wood business or to interfere with his carefully planned schedule for wood-cutting.

The relationship between landlord and tenant was more than a simple financial transaction. They were united in profiting from the land, and in protecting it. In an era before chemical fertilizers, poor farming practices, such as sowing barley directly after wheat, could exhaust the productive capacity of the soil. Knight's leases gave tenants specific directions about letting certain lands lie fallow and spreading dung on the fields as fertilizer. Tenants also had to keep farm buildings in repair. Knight typically paid for the materials (with a few exceptions, such as nails and window-glass) and paid half the labor costs for repairs, trusting the tenant to select and transport materials, hire tradesmen, and direct the work. Some projects were extensive, like the renovation of Upper Neatham Mill. In 1811, masons, carpenters, and a millwright improved the mill's main structure; thatchers and carpenters were still finishing up in 1814. The renovations cost Knight £120, while his tenant, Mary Woolveridge, had to pay a smaller share of the costs plus an additional £20 per year in rent, reflecting the mill's improved capacity.

Knight and his tenants maintained a mutually beneficial commerce, each supplying what the other lacked. Many of his tenant farmers bought firewood and building timber from him. In turn, he bought or reserved the right of first refusal to commodities they produced, such as straw and hay. At times, he contracted work out to tenants who had the equipment and labor to carry out particular projects. For example, Knight paid farmer Thomas Spencer to use his draft horses, carts, and workers to carry stones and mend the roads in Chawton Park.

The basic responsibility of the tenant was, of course, to pay rent. During difficult years, Knight allowed some of his tenants to go into arrears and, for some, excused a portion of the rent that was due; in 1816 and 1817, these write-offs of rent totaled £600. When the farmers paid their rent in 1821, he returned 15% of each payment to them. He understood the vagaries of the markets and was sympathetic to those who were struggling—but only up to a point. Knight, who had grown up watching his father run a farm in Steventon to supplement his clerical income, could tell when a farmer was in over his head. For example, he wrote to his agent, Charles Trimmer, about one tenant:

> It is very much my Wish that he should give up the Farm at Michaelmas next and I am sure it is in his interest so to do and take some smaller business whilst he has any capital left. I wish you to speak to him and his family very seriously on the subject....

Knight had no tolerance for a tenant who acted in bad faith. Like many other farmers throughout the region, Robert Hall, who rented two large farms in Steventon from Knight, got into trouble in 1815. Charles Trimmer, having received no rent, tried to work out an agreement whereby Hall would relinquish the farms in return for reimbursement of the cost of improvements Hall had made to the land. The valuation of the improvements was apparently unacceptable, however, and at Michaelmas, according to subsequent legal papers, "Hall got in his crops as usual and soon after absconded from his creditors." Knight pushed immediately for Hall's property to be seized and for Hall to be declared bankrupt. Hall owed nearly £1,000 to his creditors, including £527 to Edward Knight and £156 in tithes to the Steventon rector, James Austen. Everything Hall left on the farms, from his five cart-horses to his two silver table-spoons, was auctioned in January 1816. (Intriguingly, Mary Austen, James's wife, recorded in her diary that "Mrs. Hall" came to the Steventon rectory for dinner on the first day of the auction and stayed for two more days. There were several Halls in the Steventon area, so whether this was Robert Hall's wife, and whether he abandoned her as well as his farm, is unknown.) Finally, in 1818, Knight recovered £278 out of his total claim of £527, which did not include his legal costs or the income he lost after Hall's disappearance.

In disputes like the Hall affair, everyone lost. Knight made efforts to stay on good terms with his tenants. An important opportunity was the rent day or audit, held in December and again around midsummer. Tenant farmers paid their rent and were treated to a good dinner and plenty of liquor at a local inn. Jane Austen wrote that Knight made an effort to be at Godmersham for the rent day there. He usually settled his Hampshire accounts with his steward in the spring, but in certain years he made his visit to Chawton in the summer, and thus may have attended the audit dinners then.

Woodland Income

While rents were the most important component of a landed proprietor's income, other income-generating activities, such as farming, mining, and, most commonly, the sale of timber, provided supplemental income and flexibility. In 1811, Jane Austen walked with Henry Austen and one of his banking associates to Chawton Park Wood: "Mr. Tilson admired the trees very much," she wrote, "but grieved that they should not be turned into money."

> " ... timber in rows and avenues, which neither fashion nor extravagance had rooted up"
>
> From a description of Donwell Abbey, Emma

Turning trees into money was well understood to be one of the quickest methods by which an estate-owner could raise cash. Jane Austen, in the opening paragraphs of Sense and Sensibility, exacerbated Henry Dashwood's financial predicament (and made it more credible to her contemporary readers) by stating that he was legally prevented from selling any of the "valuable woods" on the Norland estate. An 1813 report on the scarcity of timber for Navy ships chastised landowners who "consider their woodlands to be their bankers, on whom they give drafts at sight: and when hard pressed, not merely thin the trees, but cut close as they go along." Contemporary authorities judged woodlands to be less profitable over the long term than putting the same land to the plow would be, but timber had the admirable property of standing in readiness from year to year, requiring little care until it was cut.

For Edward Knight and the Knight estate owners who preceded him, unlike many others, exploitation of the woodlands was a long-term, strategically managed business, conducted with an eye toward preservation of the woodlands as well as money-making. A large part of the pleasure Knight had in being "his own man of business," as family members observed, must have come from his steady involvement in managing his woods. Papers in the Knight archive bearing his handwriting reveal him calculating, comparing, planning. He kept and annotated a small book of maps entitled "Plan of Cuts in the Woods," and now-loose sheets show that there was at one time a separate "Beech Wood Book" as well as consolidated accounts for all of the woodland business. Money was not his only motivation: a walk around the new plantations seems to have been part of the standard entertainment for every visitor to Godmersham, and it is easy to imagine Edward Knight listening to his naval brothers' adventures and enjoying the opportunity to share his own quieter accomplishments and plans.

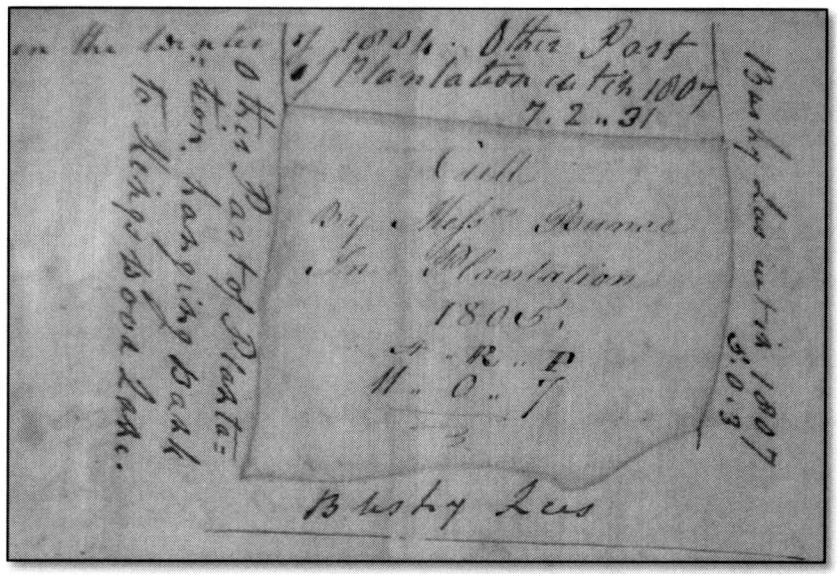

A map from the "Plan of Cuts in the Woods" book. The central map, showing the shape of a parcel of underwood "Cutt By Messrs Bunce" may have been drawn by John Bunce or Bridger Seward, Knight's steward; the darker annotations surrounding it are Edward Knight's.

Wood was harvested routinely from Chawton (where the woodlands encompassed approximately 900 acres), Steventon, and Shalden and less regularly from Neatham and Farringdon. Beech, oak, and ash were the principal trees standing in the Hampshire woodlands. The same range of wood products was sold under Edward Knight as had been sold under Elizabeth Knight, a hundred years earlier:

- **Firewood** was cut and sold in different quantities as (from largest to smallest) cordwood, faggots, and bavins, the latter two bound in bundles. Although coal was increasingly used for domestic heating (even at Chawton Great House), firewood was still in high demand in southern England. Some industries, such as brickmaking and lime-making, relied on wood for firing kilns.

- **Bark** was used in the tanning of leather. There were several tanneries in Alton.

- **Timber**, that is, wood to be sawn into planks or used whole, had a number of uses. Ash timber from Chawton was advertised as suitable for coach-makers' or wheelwrights' use, and local builders bought oak timber for house construction.

- **Hop poles** cut from slender branches were used to support hops while growing in the fields.
- **Rods,** small and flexible branches, were used to make hurdles and fencing, and for other purposes.

Timber required felling trees or topping (cutting large branches out of the crown). Firewood, hop poles, and rods were obtained through coppicing, cutting wood from a tree without killing it. Shoots would re-grow from the tree's base or stool, and after a period of years it would be ready for coppicing again. Each year, coppiced wood (known as underwood) and beech and oak timber were harvested and sold from Chawton and from Knight's other Hampshire woodlands.

A year-by-year look at wood sales solely from Chawton leads to some interesting observations. Knight relied heavily on his most renewable resource, the coppices that supplied underwood, to supplement his rental income. Felling or topping large trees was practiced much more conservatively. Knight's timber income from Chawton was greater between 1808 and 1812 than in the next few years, possibly because he needed extra cash to pay Catherine Knight's £2,000 annual stipend until her death in 1812. Then there is the enormous spike in 1819. Caroline Austen wrote in her recollections that Edward Knight was obliged to cut a "great swathe" of timber from Chawton Park to settle the Baverstock lawsuit, leaving a gap in the landscape that was visible for many years. The following chart illustrates what a radical departure this mass cutting of timber was from Knight's usual practices.

> ### SUPERIOR BEECH TIMBER.
>
> To be SOLD at AUCTION by Mr. Jeacocke, at the George Inn, Alton, on Saturday the 20th of February, 1819, at five o'clock in the afternoon, unless previously disposed of by Private Contract—110 Loads of superior round BEECH TIMBER, cut in Chawton Park, near Alton, Hants, and drawn out on the Common adjoining the Wood, from 20 to 70 foot meetings.
>
> The Timber is of extraordinary length and size, perfectly sound, and will be so allotted as to suit either dealers or consumers.
>
> Particulars of the lot, with conditions of sale, may be had of Mr. Trimmer, Alton.
>
> *Advertisement in* Hampshire Chronicle, *February 8, 1819*

Income from Sales of Timber and Underwood, 1808-1819

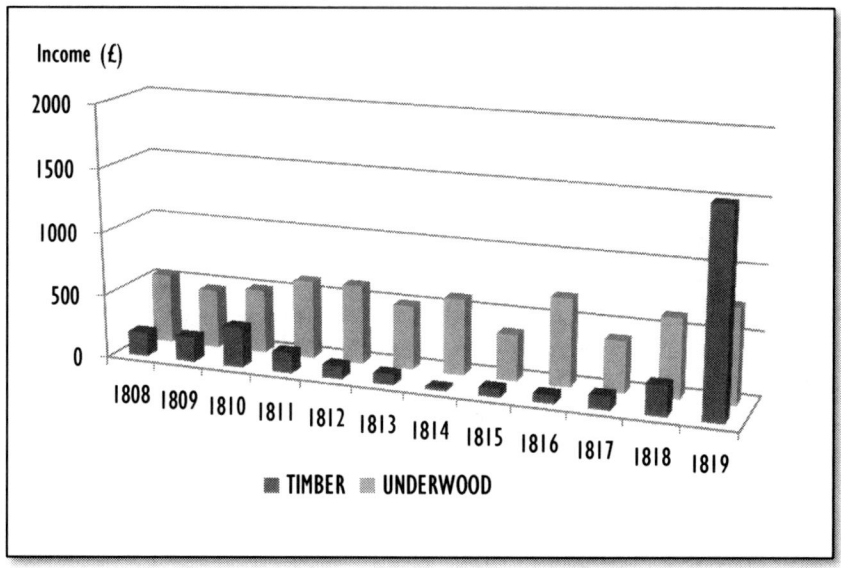

Every imaginable wood product was monetized, and woodlands were assiduously protected. Brush from trimming along the roads in the woods was sold, as were roots from land that had been cleared; even a "decayed ash" that had fallen brought £0.1.6 per foot. Diverse measures were put in place to protect the woodlands from damage and theft. Knight's laborers were often engaged in hedging the woodlands, creating a barrier to keep people and animals out. In 1801, Knight placed a notice in the *Hampshire Chronicle* forbidding sportsmen from hunting or training dogs in his woods, and his tenants (or possibly his steward, acting in their names) placed an identical notice to underscore the point. In 1808, a rash of announcements by one landowner after another appeared in the *Kentish Gazette*, declaring their woods off-limits to pigs, which were traditionally fattened on acorns. Knight was among the first to publish such a notice.[10] The newspaper printed a satirical reply to these prohibitions, titled "An humble Petition of the Pigs, to restore their ancient privilege." (It appeared, by unfortunate coincidence, directly below the announcement of Knight's wife's death.)

Edward Knight's actions to close off his woodlands were by no means unique. Rather, they reflected a widespread change in thinking that had occurred, at least among the landowning and law-making class, since the mid-18th century. In matters large and small, common property became private property, and things that had previously not been considered property at all

---

[10] *Similar notices about pigs appeared in Hampshire newspapers as well, but I have not found one issued by Edward Knight for his Hampshire woodlands. An interesting feature of many of the Hampshire notices is an additional prohibition of the collecting of hawthorn, or quick, from the woods; this plant had medicinal and culinary uses, and was also traditionally made into May Day garlands.*

were suddenly defined as such. Enclosure of common fields represented a large-scale redistribution of formerly shared land into private hands. More than 30 game laws were passed in the late 18th century, restricting who could hunt and what animals and birds were off-limits to all but certified sportsmen. Man-traps and spring-guns came into use to deter poachers (though there is no evidence in the estate accounts that they were used on Knight's land). A law passed in 1788 made gleaning[11] no longer a right but a privilege, to be awarded or withheld by landowners.

Knight would have permitted his regular workers, and perhaps some of the poorer villagers, to gather a modest amount of fallen branches and dead wood for their own hearths, but outsiders would not have been given the same privilege. Despite prohibitions, actual prosecutions for theft of wood seem to have been rare; many wood-pilferers were no doubt dealt with by local magistrates. Penalties in the cases that did reach trial were stiff, with one to three months' imprisonment typically handed down in Hampshire cases in the 1820s. Only one case was found in which Knight was named as the property owner: in 1840, a man who stole a faggot from Chawton Park Wood was sentenced to a week's imprisonment with hard labor.

Manorial Income

In *Mansfield Park*, Maria Bertram enjoys a fleeting moment of glory as the carriage party approaches her fiance's home, Sotherton Court:

> She could not carelessly observe that 'she believed it was all Mr. Rushworth's property on each side of the road,' without elation of heart; and it was a pleasure to increase with their approach to the capital freehold mansion, and ancient manorial residence of the family, with all its rights of Court Leet and Court Baron.

Maria takes pride in the great age and manorial rights of Sotherton Court, which Mansfield Park, while modern and elegant, does not possess. Similarly, Edward Knight's home at Godmersham, built in the 1730s and subsequently improved, was expansive and stylish, but Chawton had a different sort of cachet due to the history of the house, its royal associations, and its status as a manor.

The manorial system of property rights originated in Europe during the decline of the Roman Empire, when scattered landowners gained power and extended their protection to local populations. In England, manors existed among the Anglo-Saxons, but after the Norman Conquest in 1066, King William claimed the entire country for himself. He granted manors—land and associated privileges—to his supporters to reward them and bind them to him

---

[11] *Gleaning: the collection of wheat left in the fields after harvest, a traditional right of the poor.*

for military service. To his retainer Hugh De Port, the king gave Chawton and 54 other manors in Hampshire.

Each Lord of the Manor administered minor matters of the law within his manor (this was the function of the Court Leet as mentioned in *Mansfield Park*), and obtained agricultural labor by parceling out property rights in exchange. A meeting known as the Court Baron traditionally provided a way for community members and the lord's steward, jointly, to reinforce rights and rules—the customs of the manor—and to govern the use and upkeep of shared resources. The Court Baron was also the venue in which the lord's steward formalized property transactions within the manor. Each time property passed from one manorial tenant[12] to another, whether through inheritance, leasing, or sale, fees (paid in money or livestock) were due to the lord.

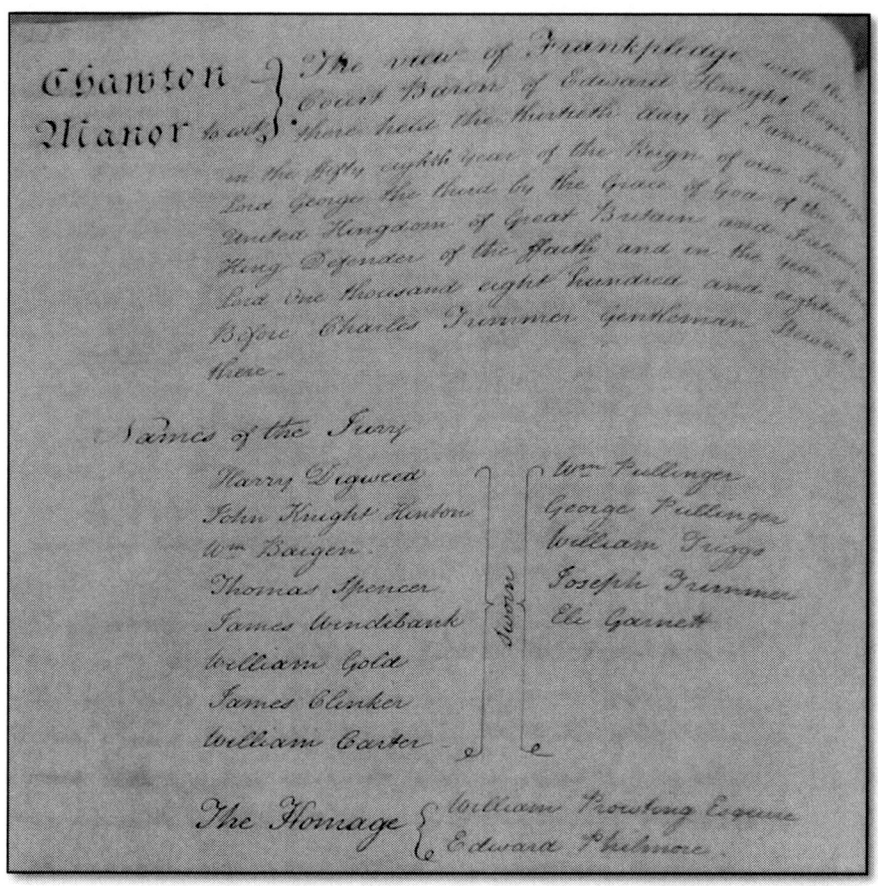

A page from the Chawton manor court book. The jury and homage of manorial tenants presented the customs of the manor, having to do with animals on the loose, maintenance of waterways, and customary footpaths. This 1818 meeting formalized the transfer of manorial tenancy from the deceased John Philmore to his son.

---

[12] *There were different types of manorial tenancy, which is not to be confused with ordinary occupation of land in exchange for market-based rent. Some forms of manorial tenancy conveyed rights virtually equivalent to actual ownership, including the ability to sell, mortgage, or leave land to one's heirs.*

In Hampshire, Edward Knight's inheritance made him Lord of the Manor[13] of Chawton, Alton Eastbrook, Truncheants, Neatham, Shalden, Steventon, and one of two manors in Farringdon. Many of the one-time manor-houses had degraded to the rank of farmhouses, and some no longer had any manor house at all, but the status or even the existence of a house had no effect on the lord's manorial rights.

Long before Edward Knight's time, the original purposes of the manorial system had become obsolete. In many places, common lands had been eliminated through enclosure, and manorial tenants' ancient obligations to plow the lord's land or serve him in battle had been replaced by cash payments. Knight and other landowners paid nominal observance to the rituals and requirements of the system, using it to protect their advantages and to collect customary fees. One type of fee that persisted past its original purpose was quit rent, an annual payment made by people holding land within a manor, including freeholders,[14] in lieu of supplying the lord with goods and services. Edward Knight collected quit rents on over 200 parcels, large and small, within his Hampshire manors. Quit rents were token payments, far less than the actual rental value of the property. Wealthy magistrate William Prowting paid £0.18.0 per year on his house and lands, while Ann Oliver paid £0.0.2 on a small cottage in Chawton that she rented out to laborers. Although the individual amounts were small, cumulatively they contributed roughly £70 a year to Knight's income. He had to pay quit rents too, amounting to about £11 each year, to lords of manors in which he had property.

All manorial fees were finally abolished in the 1920s, but manors and manorial titles still exist.[15]

Miscellaneous Income

Edward Knight's miscellaneous income varied from year to year. This category of income included occasional sales of land and, after 1813, the sale of potatoes and hay grown on the Chawton lands-in-hand. These crops were not a significant source of income, but the harvests did provide seasonal employment for villagers. For example, in 1815, 63 bushels of potatoes brought £7.1.9, and 6½ tons of hay brought £32.10.0, while the haymakers' wages totaled £17.8.6. No doubt part of the hay crop was kept for use at the Great House stables and some was used as feed for the Austen ladies' donkey.

---

[13] The title of Lord (or Lady) of the Manor was a functional description; owning a manor did not make its owner a member of the peerage.

[14] Freeholders owned their land and buildings, but were still subject to quit rents.

[15] Manorial titles without any accompanying property can be bought even now. Attempts by some newly minted Lords of the Manor to reclaim ancient rights over others' land have recently led to calls for all such rights finally to be extinguished.

Expenses

From year to year, between one-quarter and one-half of the gross earnings of Edward Knight's Hampshire estates was consumed by expenses. These expenses, as recorded in the estate accounts book, are enormously varied. Jumbled together under the "miscellaneous payments" heading are large expenses, such as the purchase of real estate, and small ones, such as a donation of a couple of shillings. Business and personal expenses were also indiscriminately mixed. Some expenses are clearly of a personal nature (such as the making of a suit for the younger Edward Knight), and others are ambiguous (such as a gunsmith's bills, which might equally have supported the gamekeeper's work or the Knight sons' play). The documentation thus presents problems for the modern researcher, even as it highlights a truth about the landed gentry in the early 19th century: the "job" of a landowner was inseparable from his identity and entitlements, and money that today would be considered business funds could be spent for personal purposes without any impropriety.

Taxes and Rates

During the period covered by the Hampshire estate accounts, taxes and rates were one of the most significant categories of expense, constituting, for example, 48% of expenses in 1810.[16] The national government collected land tax and a property and income tax, while at the parish level, "rates" were set for the support of the poor and for other purely local purposes.

Land tax: Land tax originated in 1692, and at that time valuations of property were made for the purposes of determining assessments. After 1798, the rate of taxation was fixed at £0.4.0 per pound (20%)—however, the original 1692 valuations, much lower than the actual market value of the land, were still used to determine the tax owed. Locally, farmers and tradesmen served in pairs as tax collectors. Landowners could "redeem" or excuse their property from the land tax by making a single purchase, equivalent in cost to 15 years' worth of tax, of government securities, which were intended to yield an equivalent benefit to the government. Edward Knight took this approach for some of his property, investing in redemptions even when his income was relatively low (e.g., in 1800 through 1803).

Property and income tax: Embroiled in war and plagued by instability in the currency, the government tried many different approaches to raising money in the 1790s through 1810s. A tax on income from property and professions was introduced by Prime Minister Pitt in 1799 as a temporary

---

[16] *This figure is not representative of all landowners; it reflects the low level of other expenses, due to the relatively dormant status of Knight's lands-in-hand.*

measure to help pay for the war, and was repealed in 1816. Edward Knight paid tax on his income-producing property—his rental properties and the woodlands.

Parochial rates: These are the equivalent of taxes levied and spent at the parish level. The largest of these was the Poor Rate, mandated by the Poor Law to meet the basic needs of those who could not work and to supplement the income of the working poor. (Church rates and highway rates were also levied when needed to collect money for maintenance and repairs.) The Poor Rate was based on the value of real estate, with the actual level of assessment determined by the parish vestry, a body made up of those who would pay the largest share of the rate (and thus had an incentive to set it at as low a level as possible). Nationwide, parochial rates climbed significantly over the first few decades of the 19th century as the agricultural depression led to more people depending on parish assistance and fewer solvent rate-payers. In 1774, parochial rates charged on the Hampshire portion of the Knight estates were just £14; in 1833, they reached £244. (The passage of the New Poor Law in 1834, after which date Chawton's poor were sent to Alton Workhouse, reduced the rates significantly.)

Other taxes: Miscellaneous taxes that appear in the estate records include taxes on collected quit rents, stamp duty on conveyances of deeds, and taxes on paper receipts that were drawn up when bills were paid. An embossed stamp reading "Two Pence For Receipts" appears on tradesmen's receipts in the Knight Archive, but receipts documenting payment to agricultural laborers at Chawton lack the stamp, showing that this formality was not always observed. In some years, taxes on servants and on Chawton Great House appear under the "miscellaneous" heading.

Taxes Levied on Chawton Great House, 1815

Tax on servants	£9.0.0
Tax on Great House – assessed on 66 windows	£21.0.3
Inhabited house duty	£2.16.8

Edward Knight reimbursed his tenants for the land taxes assessed on the land they rented from him. He paid parochial rates only on his woods and lands-in-hand, while his tenants paid the rates assessed on the farms they occupied. Although taxes and rates were in some years the largest category of expenses paid from the Hampshire estate revenues, Edward Knight's tax burden, and that of other landowners like him, was not large by today's standards. Especially after the end of the Napoleonic Wars, the repeal of property and income tax, along with the essentially flawed structure of the land tax, kept landowners' tax burdens modest in proportion to their income. In 1813, taxes on Knight's Hampshire property amounted to 14.8% of his gross earnings; by 1833, even with the increase in parochial rates, his overall tax burden had fallen to 5.2%.

Taxes on Knight's Hampshire Property by Type, 1808-1819

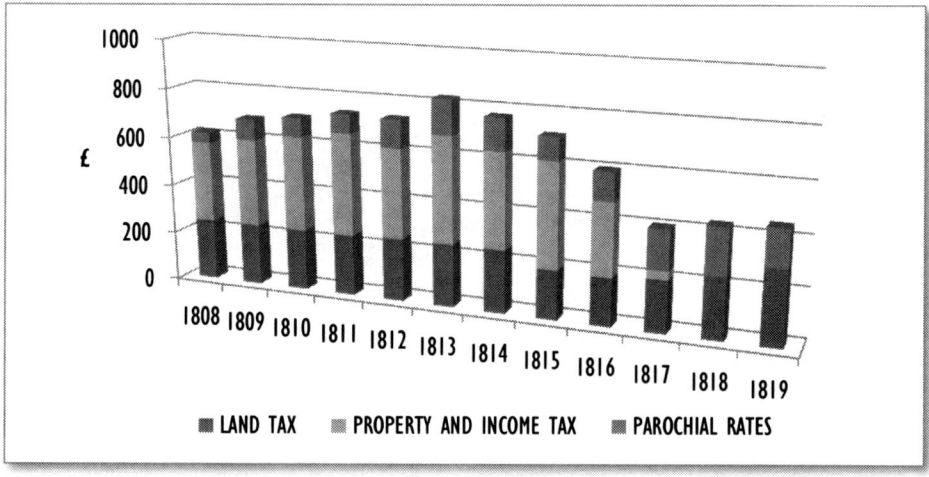

Tithes

While tithes were not strictly a tax, they functioned like one: the rector of the parish was entitled to, notionally, one-tenth of all agricultural produce and livestock raised in the parish, or the cash equivalent. In 1836, an Act of Parliament was passed to commute all tithe payments across the nation to cash, but cash payments had already been the norm in Chawton. Tithes do not appear as a separate line item in the Chawton accounts because Edward Knight's steward paid them, in cash, as each load of wood was sold, and deducted the tithe amounts before entering the sales proceeds in the estate accounts. Chawton's farmers had agreed with the rector on standard tithes to be paid per acre for the various crops they grew, but, on his wood sales, Knight paid a consistent 10% of the sale price as a tithe.

Every Farm in the Parish (except Spencers farm and the Land on the Common) to pay for every Acre and so in proportion of

Hops	£0.10.0
Wheat	0.8.0
Summer Corn	0.6.0
Meadows	0.3.0
Clover &c. cut for hay	0.2.0
Spencers Land— Wheat	0.6.0
Summer Corn	0.5.0
Clover &c. cut for hay	0.2.0

If Wheat should sink under 40s [shillings] a quarter or Barlee &c. under 20s — Mr. Hinton to sink [i.e., reduce tithes] in proportion.

Note of agreement between Chawton rector John Hinton and farmers for payment of tithes in cash, circa 1775

Insurance Fees

While the persistence of the manorial system might suggest that the business of being an estate-owner was mired in the Middle Ages, the insurance system appears, by contrast, to have been very similar to modern practices. Multiple companies offered insurance, and they appointed agents in every large town. Robert Trimmer was the Alton agent of the Hants, Sussex, and Dorset Fire Office and the Phoenix Fire Office, combining those posts with his law practice and his role as Edward Knight's agent. Knight had a fire insurance policy on the Great House (£5.8.0 per year) and another on the principal farm buildings on his rental properties. The latter policy, for which a detailed inventory of 1794 survives, provided £4,350 in coverage for an annual fee of £5.16.6.[17] Livestock insurance was also available at the time, but Knight did not carry such a policy for Chawton, since he kept very few animals there.

Expenses Directly Related to Maintaining Rental Properties

A prudent estate-owner routinely invested in the maintenance and repair of the property on which his income depended. Even when he was faced with potentially losing his Hampshire properties, Edward Knight spent money on keeping his houses, farm buildings, and hedges in good condition. His investment in this area dipped in 1816 and 1817, but the next two years more than made up for the short period of lower spending. Payments for repairs listed in the accounts book include work done to Chawton Great House and Mrs. Austen's cottage—both of which straddled the line between rental properties and personal homes at various times. There are issues with the data on repairs in the accounts book, but, taking the figures as given, between 1808 and 1819, approximately 12% of Knight's gross earnings from his Hampshire properties was directed toward repairs.

Payments for Repairs

Year	1808	1809	1810	1811	1812	1813	1814	1815	1816	1817	1818	1819
£	287	286	324	380	884	796	731	655	324	421	1,232	1,021

Expenses Directly Related to Selling Wood Products

The following chart is a notional view of the costs and profits involved in selling timber and underwood, based on data derived from a number of records in the Knight archive. The chart is not intended to represent all sales, or any one particular sale (as none of the available examples provided exact figures for all of these cost elements), but rather to facilitate a comparison of relative costs. Some costs were standardized: the steward or woodman who

---

[17] *Valuations of some of the farm buildings covered under this policy appear in the next chapter.*

arranged the sale earned 5% commission, and the rector's tithe on wood sold was 10%. Other costs were highly variable: transport costs, for example, were zero if timber was sold standing, as it often was. The transport costs in this example come from 1794 sales records: 16% of the gross revenue from that year's wood sales was consumed by the cost of transporting sold wood, while labor costs (for harvesting only, not including planting and maintaining the growing trees) represented only 14%. Transportation was very expensive, labor very cheap.

Expenses Related to Sales of Wood

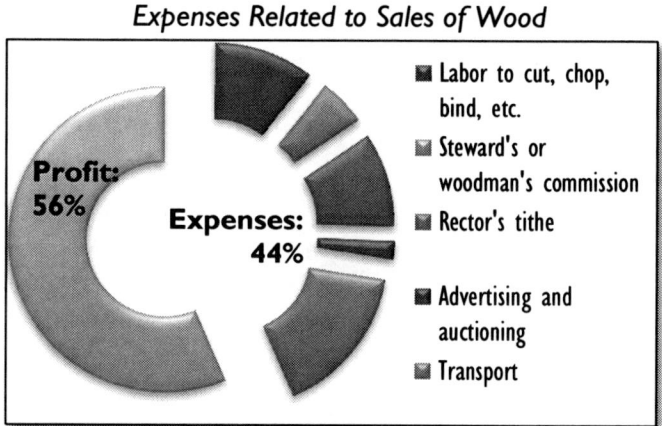

For each of his wood-producing manors, Knight engaged a woodman, on a modest annual salary, to watch over his woods and supervise work in them. Knight kept his labor costs low by employing a small number of day-laborers to work in his woodlands as needed, rather than hiring workers by the year. The day-laborers nurtured and planted seedlings and maintained the estate infrastructure by hedging around parcels of land and maintaining the roads and paths in the woods. Much of their effort was directed toward harvesting and preparing wood products to be sold: this included cutting timber and underwood, chopping and binding wood intended for hearth or kiln, and peeling bark.

The wages Knight paid his workers in the woods were comparatively good: his standard daily wage was £0.2.0, one-third more than the average farm-worker's wage in England's predominantly agricultural counties, according to authorities of the time. For certain tasks, Knight paid £0.2.6 or £0.2.8, reflecting the higher skill level required for work such as hedge-making. Day-laborers generally did not receive lodging or food from their employer. The only recorded benefits that Knight's gave his workers were "wood money" and "beer money," traditional small gratuities given when certain tasks were performed (beside one such expense appears the note "customary on barking the oak").

Other Estate Management Expenses

The salary of Knight's steward or agent, at £120.0.0 per year, was a major expense supporting all aspects of estate ownership. Knight also paid salaries to a small staff of estate servants who were hired in 1813 to keep the house and grounds in readiness for the Knight family's visits.

An estate-owner who operated a home farm would have a number of farm servants—plowmen, shepherds, carters, stable-workers, and so on—whom he would employ by the year and might house on the estate. Knight had such workers at Godmersham Park, but the low level of agricultural operations at Chawton did not require them.

The Special Role of the Estate-Owner: More than Making Money

Any discussion of the estate economy that merely compared income and expenses would be incomplete. The landowner was not a wage-earner whose accomplishments and stability could be measured simply by the money he made, nor a merchant or business-owner who could readily sell up in one place and set up elsewhere. Instead, he was the beneficiary of the decisions and actions of those who held the estate before him, and the trustee of the property that would be handed to future heirs. The power of that responsibility is seen in *Persuasion*: Sir Walter Elliot, not the most attentive landowner in any other respect, "would never disgrace his name" by selling part of his estate; though not particularly close to his heir, Sir Walter would nonetheless transfer Kellynch "whole and entire, as he had received it."

Landowners who could or would not sell their land could raise cash by mortgaging it. Edward Knight mortgaged property as a crisis-management approach, not, as Sir Walter Elliot did, to fund continual excesses in "journeys, London, servants, horses, table." Jane Austen witnessed the dissolution of an estate and the ruination by debt of a family she knew well: the Harwoods of Deane House. In 1813, John Harwood VI died, and it emerged that he had gotten deeply into debt and mortgaged everything he could. His heir, John Harwood VII, could not afford to marry and spent his life trying to recover from his father's folly, while his younger brother Charles sank to the state of a yeoman farmer.

Improving the Estate

Maintenance and improvement of the estate seems to have always been in Edward Knight's mind. Almost as soon as he came into control of the Knight property, and when his cash position was not yet strong, he began to work on improving its land holdings. In 1803, he exchanged some property in Chawton village with another landowner, acquiring a malt house, two cottages, and some land near the Great House. He exchanged two acres of land with William Prowting, the local magistrate, for their mutual convenience. He also bought a small piece of land from Prowting, making the fields of New Park Farm more contiguous.

> ## "The land was so very desirable for me in every respect, so immediately adjoining my own property, that I felt it my duty to buy it."
>
> *John Dashwood in* Sense and Sensibility

His strategic land sales and purchases continued. In 1811, he sold his property in Winchester, preferring to consolidate his holdings in the area around Chawton. In 1815 and 1816, he sustained heavy losses from Henry Austen's business failure and faced the possibility of losing his Hampshire properties due to the Baverstock lawsuit. In those same years, however, the price of farmland fell, and he took the opportunity to buy more land in Kent, despite having to mortgage part of it almost immediately.[18]

In 1818, Knight mortgaged his property in Farringdon, adjacent to Chawton, and at Buckwell in Kent.[19] At the same time, his expenditures on repairing and improving his Hampshire properties peaked, exceeding £1,000 in both 1818 and 1819. That he was able to cope with enormous losses and still invest in improvements is evidence of his business acumen and his dedication to the concept of the enduring estate.

Another area in which attention to long-term impacts was important was the cultivation and exploitation of the woodlands. In 1748, Thomas Knight's steward, Edward Randall, had written to his employer, offering options for using Chawton Park Wood and projecting the long-term financial impact of each. Randall warned that much of the woodland "is thin enough now" and that it might all be cut in just 15 years. One of his recommended options was clearing only 20 acres a year and allowing the woodland to reestablish itself. Such conservative usage is consistent with the way Edward Knight used the land a half-century and more later. Knight maintained a strict schedule for harvesting coppice wood, and only financial extremity made him exceed moderate felling of his timber woods. In addition, he made new plantations at both Chawton and Godmersham.

---

[18] *One of these purchases, the Pontus estate, deserves more investigation. It was secured by a deed of trust to Knight's brothers, Francis and Charles Austen. It is possible that he made the purchase on their behalf, as an investment of their naval prize money.*

[19] *The information on these two properties comes from lawyers' bills. Other mortgages may also have been executed, as noted in the Appendix.*

Community Investment and Philanthropy

The estate owner's responsibilities extended beyond his own family and posterity. If the account summary Edward Knight's agent prepared for him each year were a 21st-century corporate annual report, it might include a section titled "Corporate Social Responsibility." Jane Austen's letters mention her and Cassandra's plans for spending the £10 that Knight put into their hands each year so that they could provide small comforts for poor villagers, but his support for the community went much further.

Knight gave an Alton apothecary and surgeon £10 a year to attend the poor. The Chawton Overseers of the Poor were charged with securing adequate medical care for those without means, and their records show that they did indeed summon doctors for all sorts of illnesses, but Knight's contribution bridged the gap between the need and the overseers' budget. Knight also made contributions to the county hospital.

In the 1780s, Thomas Knight I built six tenements for "the accommodation of such old and necessitous inhabitants of this parish that are not themselves able to pay any rent for their houses." In 1817, Edward Knight built two more, at a cost of more than £150. The parish officers paid him a nominal rent, £1.0.0 a year per cottage. At that rate, it would have taken him quite a long time to recoup his investment, so it seems safe to say that profit was not his motive.

A "poor school" for village children had operated in Chawton at least since 1788 and probably well before,[20] which Edward Knight continued to support. Ann Browning, the schoolmistress, received a salary of £10 a year, which Knight raised to £15 in 1812. She also taught the girls' class at Sunday school, for which she received an additional £5 paid by various contributors including Edward Knight and, while she lived, Catherine Knight. Village schools were without a doubt imperfect. All ages were lumped together in the same class, and the teacher's own education might be very basic. In 1788, the schoolmistress taught the Chawton children reading and needlework, but not writing; Ann Browning, a couple of decades later, may have been more capable. A particularly promising boy might be sent on to Eggar's free grammar school at Alton. Occasionally a bright girl was noticed: Jane Austen wrote in 1813 that Harriet Knight, daughter of laborer Abraham Knight, came every day to read to Cassandra Austen.

An 1819 government survey of educational resources in England shows that Chawton, along with Steventon, was more fortunate than many villages in having schools regularly funded by the principal landowner. The parishes of

---

[20] *A 1788 document in the Knight archive, a copy of the Chawton rector's responses to a bishop's questionnaire reads, "The children of the poor are taught to read and work [i.e., do needlework] supported chiefly by the annual bounty of Thomas Knight." The schoolmistress then was Ann Stacey.*

Shalden and Farringdon—in both of which Knight also owned extensive property—had no provisions for basic education. Shalden's minister wrote in his response to the survey that:

> The poor are without the means of educating their children, and they have very little time to attend to education, except on Sundays, being employed from a very early age in agriculture. A Sunday school has been lately relinquished from the failure of means to support it, but the minister hopes soon to re-establish it.

A village day school, 1804.

Knight made various small, customary donations. At Christmas, the bell ringers at the Church of St. Nicholas received £1.1.0, the parish clerk got £0.10.0, and poor women, varying in number from five to nine, each received £0.5.0. A gratuity of £0.2.6 was given to the men who walked the boundaries of the parish on Ascension Day.

In addition to his institutionalized giving to the Chawton community, Knight and his family made efforts to tend to the needs of individuals. Fanny Knight wrote in her diary of making visits to the poor with her mother during their first visit to Chawton in 1807. Cassandra and Jane Austen took on this duty when the Knight family was not present.

Looking just at 1810 as an example, expenses for charity and community support in the Hampshire estate accounts represent 2% of expenses and not quite 1% of net profits for that year.[21] This is not out of step with modern standards: the median amount given to charity in 2012 by a group of 106 of the top revenue-producing companies in the U.S. was 0.8% of pre-tax profits. Still, there were persistent inequities, and some of the actions of people 200 years ago can be difficult to reconcile. Time and again, instances of generosity toward one person or group contrast with what appears to be a lack of recognition of the equally urgent needs of others.

---

[21] *The estate accounts only reflect money that passed through Knight's agent's hands.*

One anecdote will suffice. Samuel Smith, a wealthy farmer (who had rented a large farm from Edward Knight) unwisely went into business as a brewer, lost all his money, and "sank under his difficulties," leaving destitute a widow and 14 children, ranging from infancy to the age of 27. A collection was organized to provide for the family, to which Knight donated £50. Mrs. Smith's case was seen as so desperate that other less-than-wealthy widows contributed, including Mrs. Austen, who gave £2.2.0. In all, £827 was collected, and Mrs. Smith was assisted in setting up a boarding-house. When she and her eldest daughter died two years later, a second collection was begun for the surviving children. In contrast, the most a laborer's widow in Chawton might receive was a flannel petticoat and a few shillings at Christmas. In *Emma*, pork and apples and regular hot dinners at Donwell and Hartfield sustain Miss and Mrs. Bates (daughter and widow of a clergyman, just as Jane Austen and her mother were)—but for the poor cottagers that Emma and Harriet visit, compassion and broth do little to relieve their poverty and sickness.

> It was pleasing to hear him speak so properly; here he had been acting as he ought to do. To be the friend of the poor and the oppressed! Nothing could be more grateful to her ...
>
> *Fanny Price reflecting on Henry Crawford, Mansfield Park*

Both of these examples, real and fictional, reflect the values of the time. People who had money and lost it often elicited more sympathy and greater help than those who had never had much money to begin with. Statistician and social theorist Patrick Colquhoun considered poverty no evil; he deemed it "a most necessary and indispensable ingredient in society, without which nations and communities could not exist in a state of civilization." The proper role of parish support and philanthropy, he asserted, was merely to "prop up" those who were completely indigent through no fault of their own and restore them to a state of poverty, where need would spur them on to labor. He was by no means alone in these views. The social complexity and contradictions we see in Jane Austen's novels, particularly in *Emma* and *Mansfield Park,* existed in Chawton in the early 19th century. Despite inconsistencies, the level of Edward Knight's community support—including the wages he paid, steps he took to keep farmers in business (and thus able to employ workers and pay poor rates), and his support for health care and education—enabled the Chawton community to avoid the depths of desperation seen in many villages in southern England at the time.

5. Estate and Community

Two scraps of paper in the Knight Archive provide a snapshot of Chawton society on Sunday mornings. Sketched in pencil, they are plans, with slight variations, of the principal pews in the Church of St. Nicholas and the families to whom they are assigned.[22]

In the front pews are the families of Edward Knight and William Prowting, the squire and the magistrate respectively. Mrs. Austen and her daughter Cassandra, by virtue of their relationship to Knight, sit in the second row, along with Martha Lloyd. Behind them is the family of Captain Benjamin Clement, gentleman, who is married to Mr. Prowting's daughter, Ann-Mary. Three of Edward Knight's farming tenants and their families sit on the left: Harry Digweed, who farms more than 500 acres and whose wife is of a Hampshire gentry family; James Windibank of New Park Farm, recently widowed; and Thomas Spencer, tenant of Knight's smallest farm. William Baigen, seated with Spencer, rents a farm from a different landlord and also has land of his own. The pew across the aisle seats William Gold, mason. James Clinker, blacksmith, and Edward Philmore, who has a shop, are in the next row. Knight's servants from the Great House sit together in a pair of short pews. At the pulpit is the rector, John-Rawstorne Papillon.

The recollections of Chawton resident John White help to fill in a bit more of the scene.[23] William Carter, the parish clerk, sits in the front gallery, along

	Pulpit	
Mr. Knight		Mr. Prowting
Digweed		Mrs. Austen
Windibank		Capt. Clement
Baigen & Spencer		Mr. Gold
Philmore & Clinker		GH Servants
		GH Servants

Transcript of an undated sketch of Chawton church pew assignments.

---

[22] In the second sketch, the places for Philmore and Clinker and some of the Great House servants are switched. While a plan similar to these would probably have been drawn in preparation for the Knights' five-month visit to Chawton in 1813, these sketches most likely date from 1820, when the Knight family made another extended stay at the Great House. James Windibank first appeared on Knight's rent list in 1818; everyone else named on the sketch had lived in Chawton since 1812 or earlier.

[23] John White was born in 1821, and nearly 100 years later dictated his memories of his childhood in Chawton.

The original Church of St. Nicholas with the Great House in the background, 18th-century painting. The present church is the result of Victorian rebuilding after a devastating fire.

with the singers, and leads the congregants in their responses during the service. William Goodchild, the thatcher, sits in the back gallery; he serves as the parish's sexton (gravedigger) and teaches Sunday school to boys in the village. Abraham Knight, a laborer in the Chawton woodlands, may be found in the church tower, ringing the bells.

Other villagers find their places elsewhere in the church. Here are rich and poor, rate-payers and recipients of charity, sometimes with the same surname. James Windibank has his pew up front, while Thomas Windibank, one of the most frequent recipients of parish relief, crowds into the gallery with the rest of the laborers. Also among the poor villagers are the Garnetts, whose orderly and attractive children Jane Austen looked upon with approval, and the Whites, who struggle because the father, a veteran of the Battle of Waterloo, is unable to work.

This was Chawton—roughly 70 families, inhabiting some 40 houses. Most families were employed in agriculture, either as farmers or laborers.[24] Much of the community was linked economically to the Great House in some way, but a smaller proportion of the property in the village was owned by the Knight estate than would be the case later in the 19th century, and only a handful of people worked day-to-day on the estate.

The preceding chapter focused on the estate economy from the point of view of the landowner, as personified by Edward Knight. This chapter explores

---

[24] An 1811 government survey reported 56 households employed in agriculture and four in trade; eight families were classified as "other."

the lives of other people who participated in that economy: their work, financial security, social mobility, prestige, contributions to the community, and family life, as well as their interactions with Knight and his family. Jane Austen would have known most of the people profiled in this chapter—though she socialized with few, she mentioned many of them in her letters. By learning about them, we learn more about her and about the dimly seen, seldom-heard non-gentry figures that populate the background of her novels.

I have grouped the people described in this section into categories. While this sort of structure may be helpful to the reader, it is important not to consider such labels as rigid and static. People who earned income by renting land to others—the landed proprietors—remained firmly at the top of the social structure of the early 19th century, but the agricultural distress in the first three decades increased social mobility (upward and downward) among farmers and decreased the importance of distinctions between tenant-farmers and yeomen, those who farmed their own land. Similarly, opportunity determined whether a person was a day-laborer or a farm servant hired by the year; many farm servants slipped down to the status of day-laborers, and some went in the other direction. In general, tradesmen's work practices, level of literacy, and degree of financial independence were superior to those of farm servants and laborers, but to each apparent rule, exceptions exist.

The Squire and His Surrogates

The squire, or principal landowner in a parish, is a familiar character in English fiction, including Jane Austen's. Mr. Musgrove, in *Persuasion*, and Sir John Middleton, in *Sense and Sensibility*, resemble the stereotypical 18th-century country squire: bluff, sociable, devoted to country life, and not particularly cultured. Austen's description of Lady Catherine de Bourgh, the rare female landowner, reflects another aspect of a squire's role:

> Though this great lady was not in the commission of peace for the county, she was a most active magistrate in her own parish ... and whenever any of the cottagers were disposed to be quarrelsome, discontented, or too poor, she sallied forth into the village to settle their differences, silence their complaints, and scold them into harmony and plenty.

Many country squires served as magistrates and justices of the peace—Mr. Knightley in *Emma* is another fictional example. The squire was felt to have a certain moral authority, whether it was exercised formally through the justice system, or with the personal touch of a Lady Catherine. Parties to disputes often laid their cases before the squire to resolve (an echo, no doubt, of the manorial Court Leet where the Lord of the Manor would adjudicate tenants' disagreements). Constables who apprehended offenders would bring them to the magistrate's home, where he would dispense summary judgment in minor matters or order those suspected of crimes to be held for trial. A subset of the magistrates within the county tried more serious matters at the quarterly assizes, handing down sentences that included imprisonment, hard labor, transportation, and death. The moral authority of the squire cut both ways: the squire was felt to have a special duty to sponsor festivities for the community on appropriate occasions, give extra help to the poor in times of bad weather, and take care of community problems when no one else would. For example, Edward Randall, steward to Thomas Knight I, wrote to him about the railings at the churchyard in Alton, stating that "it is said to belong to you to repair"; no one remembered quite why it was Knight's responsibility, but the steward strongly hinted he should take care of it anyway. Many decades later, Edward Knight stepped into the breach at Godmersham to feed a crowd of itinerant laborers who had come to the district hoping to be hired to build the new railway. Knight was strongly opposed to the railway, but would not see its workers starve at his gates.

So what happened when the squire was absent, as Knight was from Chawton most of the time and from Steventon all of the time? Surrogates took on some parts of the squire's role, and other parts went unfulfilled. William Prowting, Chawton's second most prominent citizen, served as the magistrate for many years. The parson became more important: in *Mansfield Park*, because there is no squire near Edmund Bertram' parsonage at Thornton Lacey, his "privilege and independence" are felt to be greater, and his responsibilities would be, too. The squire's principal tenant often became a quasi-squire, enjoying his landlord's deputation to shoot game and extending a watchful eye and helpful hand over the village. At Steventon, the Digweeds, longstanding tenants, gained prestige as surrogates of the Knights and occupants of what remained of the Tudor manor house.

During Edward Knight's ownership, his tenants at the Great House were John-Charles Middleton in 1795 and again from 1808 through early 1813, and Thomas Coulthard from 1800 to 1807. Frank Austen and his family lived there in 1815. In 1816, plans seem to have been made for some relatives of the Chawton rector to take the house for a time; servants moved in to prepare it, but events in Kent intervened, and Jane Austen, who no doubt had been dreading compulsory dinners and visits with the new tenants, celebrated "the happy end of the Kentish Papillons coming here."

In 1825, Knight again made plans to rent out the Great House. Nothing came of it, but in contemplating the idea, Knight made notes about what the house offered, with particular attention to the dimensions of the drawing room, dining room, gentleman's room, and dressing closet. A further ten master bedrooms were available, and there were five bedrooms for maidservants and another five for male servants in the house, as well as two rooms over the stables.

A squire meeting with a tenant, 1799. Squire: "Come my good friend, here is to your health! Why don't you draw nearer?" Tenant: "I don't know—but I always feels as it were stounded when I sits in company with your Honor's Glory."

Knight drafted an advertisement:

Mr. Knight is willing to let for a year from the 29th September 1825 Chawton House with the furniture, Stables, coach houses, Kitchen Garden, Pleasure Grounds, and 14 Acres of Meadow Ground, in the whole about 30 Acres of land, including a Right of sporting over upwards of 3,000 acres in the parishes of Chawton and Farringdon. Mr. K will continue to pay the present Game Keeper, Gardener, Yard Man and his Wife the Dairy Woman their Wages as at present, he will also pay all Parochial rates, House [tax], Window Tax, and Tithes. He will do all the necessary Repairs to the House except Glass to the Windows and Garden Frames.

It is easy to envision Mr. Bingley in *Pride and Prejudice*, or Admiral Croft in *Persuasion*, perusing such an advertisement. We can imagine Mr. Bingley focusing on the excellent sporting possibilities of the property. The ability to leave the outdoor work in the hands of servants already in place would have appealed to the Admiral, who had little experience of life on land.

ᔌ Genteel Tenants: John-Charles Middleton and Family

Just as Charles Bingley "sometimes made choice of his county" but "might leave the next generation to purchase" an estate, so John-Charles Middleton was a long-term renter. In addition to Chawton Great House, over the years he took various other houses in Hampshire and Surrey, including, in 1789, the newly built mansion at Hinton Ampner. In an 1813 letter, Jane Austen passed on to Cassandra the news that Middleton "will really try for a house" of his own, but it was not to be: Middleton moved back to Shawford House, near Winchester, which he had rented before coming to Chawton Great House. He spent his final years at Hildersham in Cambridgeshire.

Middleton had come to Hampshire after a career in India. He was a brother or perhaps a nephew to Nathaniel Middleton, who worked for and later became the chief witness in the trial of Warren Hastings, Governor General of India. John-Charles Middleton was a widower by the time he came to Chawton. During his years at the Great House, his sister-in-law, Maria Beckford, and his six children lived with him. One of those children, Charlotte-Maria, would in later life seek out James-Edward Austen-Leigh's *A Memoir of Jane Austen* and subsequently write her own recollections of her youth in Chawton.

In *Persuasion*, part of Sir Walter Eliot's decision to accept Admiral Croft as a tenant depends on his approval of the social relationship that will naturally follow on from the financial one between them. Similarly, the Middletons were acquainted not only with the Knights, but also with the Austens, and remained so for years. The female inhabitants of the Great House and the Austen ladies visited back and forth (though at times, Jane Austen was "very glad to escape" the visitors); Susan Middleton and Fanny Knight spent time together whenever the latter visited Chawton. Maria Beckford and the eldest Miss Middleton happened to be in London in 1811 and were invited to Henry and Eliza Austen's musical party, and three years later, after the Middletons had left Chawton, Jane Austen made a point of calling on Maria Beckford in London. Jane's nephew James-Edward Austen-Leigh, at a party in 1820, chatted with Maria and Lucy Middleton ("by far the finest girls in the room") and listened to their reminiscences of childhood fun at the Great House.

John-Charles Middleton tried his hand at being a gentleman farmer in a minor way. At the expiration of his lease, Edward Knight paid Middleton for the remainder of the hay and potatoes that he (or more precisely his servants) had grown. Jane Austen criticized either his skill or his luck, observing that Middleton never had a hay crop in five years to equal Knight's in 1813. Middleton made an effort to contribute to the community, giving a guinea toward Ann Browning's annual salary of £5.5.0 for teaching at the Sunday School. Whether his sister-in-law and children made visits of charity in the village is unknown, but they did extend the hospitality of the Great House to Elizabeth Benn, a poor spinster who is known from Jane Austen's letters.

The Steward

In the pages of Jane Austen's novels are several examples of the men who helped landed proprietors manage their estates. William Larkins, the bailiff for Donwell Abbey in *Emma*, meets with Mr. Knightley every week to go over the farm accounts. Mr. Morris makes a fleeting appearance on the first page of *Pride and Prejudice*, striking the rental agreement that makes Mr. Bingley the tenant of Netherfield Park. In the same novel, Mr. Wickham's late father, trained as a lawyer, "had the management of all the Pemberley estates." Another lawyer, Mr. Shepherd in *Persuasion*, is the agent for Sir Walter Elliot's estate business. In *Mansfield Park*, Dr. Grant employs a bailiff to manage his glebe land, and Sir Thomas Bertram, whose attentions are largely diverted to his concerns in Antigua, has both a bailiff and a steward at Mansfield. In *Northanger Abbey*, General Tilney's steward draws him away from Bath with a letter about urgent business.

A *bailiff* was a farm manager. A *steward* occupied a more responsible position than a bailiff; in addition to overseeing agricultural operations, a steward would collect rents, deal with tenants, give advice, and represent the landowner in the latter's absence. An agricultural survey in 1810 placed the average bailiff's annual salary at £30; Edward Knight paid his steward £120 per year. *Steward* and *agent* are roughly synonymous, though agents (who were often lawyers) generally had little or no involvement in directing agricultural operations.

There were no uniform requirements for a steward's background or skills. When Elizabeth Knight hired John Heath as her steward in 1702, having heard good reports of his "Honesty, Integrity, & Understanding in Woods," she gave him responsibility for looking after the woodlands, administering the accounts of wood cut and bricks made on the estate, collecting rents, and generally overseeing all of her business in Hampshire. Edward Randall and his son, who worked in succession for Thomas Knight I from 1738 to 1774, brought experience as surveyors to the job and had the mathematical and analytical ability to develop long-term projections of income from the Chawton woodlands. Bridger Seward, who was hired by Thomas Knight II and continued to work for Thomas's wife Catherine and then for Edward Knight, was a successful farmer. Notably absent from Seward's duties was presiding over the manorial Court Baron; during his tenure, Knight engaged lawyers for that purpose, including Robert Trimmer, an attorney and solicitor with offices in Alton and Farnham.

A farmer wearing a smock meets with an estate steward, who is surrounded by maps, rent lists, and accounts, 1799. Farmer: "Donna look so glum your Honor—I would pay my Rent un I could, but consider what a nation bad hay time it has been."

When Seward died in 1808, Trimmer took over as agent for all of Knight's Hampshire affairs while continuing to carry on with legal work for other clients and represent two fire insurance companies. When Robert Trimmer died in 1813, his son Charles stepped into his shoes as lawyer and agent; in the 1820s, Charles branched out further, renting farmland from Knight and becoming a banker for a time.[25] For the next century, members of the Trimmer family continued to manage the Knights' estate affairs.

Whatever his background, a steward had to manage a broad range of activities. He was responsible for planning and overseeing the work done on his employer's lands-in-hand, interacting directly with laborers. He collected

---

[25] *It appears that Trimmer, in his capacity as a banker, was involved in making loans to Edward Knight in the 1820s (see the Appendix for details).*

rents, kept an eye on tenants' use of leased property, and authorized and paid for repairs. He paid taxes and rates, and kept an eye on issues in the county and the parish that could have an impact on the landowner's affairs. He managed all the estate's records, including maps, leases, insurance policies, records of income, vouchers and receipts, and (in Knight's case) long-term plans for estate lands. A successful steward had to know how to evaluate and manage people: he had to select tradesmen and laborers, determine whether the bills and work vouchers presented to him were credible, decide when tenants deserved leniency, and attract and negotiate with prospective tenants.

During Seward's and the Trimmers' tenure, management of the Hampshire estates was simpler and conducted on a more businesslike footing than it had been in the 18th century. Part of John Heath's job in the early 1700s was to sell firewood to many individual buyers, but Seward and the Trimmers generally sold large lots by auction or dealt with middlemen. John Heath also supervised the brickworks at Chawton, but that operation was inactive by the early 19th century. Edward Randall, who lived in Chawton Great House to oversee it when Thomas Knight I was not visiting, was responsible for feeding and watching over Knight's servants there, and, as Knight testily reminded him, he received considerable benefits in return:

> You have the keeping of two Cows [wrote Knight], you have all Firing, Beer, & Use of Furniture for yourself & Family, you have things necessary out of the Garden, & the Profit of the Pidgeon House, & keeping a Horse &c, all which if you did not live in the House, to keep the other Servants there, I should have no occasion to allow to a Steward....

The stewards and agents who followed Randall were kept at more of a distance, as were the estate servants.

Edward Knight advised his son and heir to "manage your own affairs as much as you can, and have frequent settlements with any Agents you may employ." That is what he did himself. Knight traveled to Chawton at least twice a year to meet with his agent and go over the books; no expense was too small to be listed in the accounts and backed up by a signed receipt. If employers were less diligent, however, stewards and agents were well-placed to steer business affairs in the direction that was most advantageous to themselves, or even to cheat their employers. Elizabeth Knight dismissed John Heath's predecessor for setting up his own brickworks when he was being paid for managing hers. In *Mansfield Park*, Henry Crawford worries that his steward, Maddison, is working against his best interests by trying to secure the lease of a mill for a friend of his. In *Persuasion*, Mr. Shepherd clearly manipulates Sir Walter Elliot and acts behind his back, though arguably his actions to sell Sir Walter on the move to Bath and find a tenant for Kellynch Hall are for Sir Walter's own good. The importance of an honest and capable manager acting in the landowner's interests is shown in *Pride and Prejudice* by the late

Mr. Darcy's high regard for his steward and the consequent favor shown to the steward's son, George Wickham.

❧ Steward and Farmer: Bridger Seward

The small room at the back of Jane Austen's House Museum, now used as a reading room, has historically been called the "office," and it is easy to envision Bridger Seward, Edward Knight's steward for his Hampshire estates, stationed there. The steward would have possession of many important papers and keep cash on hand, and it is notable that the windows of that room, and no other in the house, are fitted with iron bars. Just a few steps away are outbuildings where tools would have been stored; from the small office, Seward could keep an eye on laborers coming and going. People coming to do business with him could enter the office by its own door and avoid disturbing Seward's wife and daughters, at home in the rest of the house.

There had been a designated "steward's room" at Chawton Great House in the mid-18th century, but, when the Great House was rented out to tenants, the bustle of the steward's activities and the traffic of tradesmen and farmers would have been undesirable. Seward and his family had moved into the cottage in 1788. From there, he managed not only Knight's property but his own farming activities. Seward owned 25 acres in Chawton, and held 18 acres by manorial tenancy in Farringdon. In Chawton, he leased two farms from Edward Knight, Pound Farm and Lower Farm, and later added on a smaller parcel of property called "Tanner's Land" from Knight and a bit more from another landlord. He grew hops, among other crops, and raised sheep. No record of his income has been found, but he was clearly financially comfortable. When Seward died suddenly in 1808, he left £200 and his household goods to his wife, £800 to his adult daughter by his first wife, and £1,000 each to his four minor daughters.

Seward was not Knight's largest tenant, but he had standing in the community independent of his role as steward. In 1786, he was on the committee directing the "Association of the Town of Alton, & parts adjacent" to encourage the prosecution of thieves and vandals. In 1797, he joined with other "occupiers of land" near Alton who wanted to establish a sheep fair there and promised to bring their stock to it. In 1807, he participated in a dual role at a meeting of landowners and occupiers opposing plans to build a canal: he was named on the list of prominent gentlemen as Edward Knight's representative, and he also appeared on his own behalf on the list of the less august participants. He was appointed to the committee to lead the opposition, along with a baron and baronet, two esquires, and two clergymen; he almost certainly would not have gotten such an appointment on his own merit, but was included as Knight's representative.

An interaction between the women of the Knight and Seward families illustrates their relative social positions. In September 1807, during their first stay at Chawton Great House, Edward Knight's wife Elizabeth and her daughter Fanny called on Mrs. Seward on three occasions. On their second visit, they asked to borrow the Sewards' pianoforte, which was delivered to the Great House that afternoon. Mrs. Seward (née Mary Duncombe) was respectable enough to be visited—she rated a mention in *Burke's Genealogical and Heraldic History of Commoners of Great Britain* as being "descended from an ancient Surrey family"—but her husband's position as Knight's employee made the family decidedly inferior.

For the most part, Seward's estate accounts and correspondence are not available (although some may exist in the portion of the Knight Archives that cannot be accessed without significant conservation work). One document in his hand that does survive is a summary of wood sold in 1803. It is carefully prepared, neatly laying out the acreage and location of the wood cut, the expenses of cutting and chopping, the names of buyers and the price paid, and deductions for the rector's tithe and Seward's own 5% commission on sales. Given Seward's standing in the community and his apparent competence (judging from the scant available documentation), we may wonder why Edward Knight chose to replace him not with another farmer, but with a lawyer from the nearby town. Possibly Knight, at something of a disadvantage as an absentee landlord, wanted a steward who had fewer personal ties to the tenant farmers and was less liable to be distracted by his own farming concerns.

Estate Servants and Farm Servants

Estate servants cared for woodlands, gardens, and sporting grounds, whereas farm servants tended animals and cultivated crops. These servants were distinguished from day-laborers by being engaged by an employer for a defined period, usually a year, and receiving a set wage or salary for that time. This distinction is reflected in Edward Knight's estate accounts book, in which his estate servants' wages are recorded separately from payments to laborers.

Estate and farm servants often lived rent-free in rooms provided by their employer, and some were provided food by their employer as well.

Study of a woodcutter from an undated collection of figure studies by Robert Hills (1769-1844).

57

Many day-laborers aspired to these more secure positions, and, as the example of Abraham Knight later in this section shows, some of them succeeded. Taking such a position meant being bound by a contract, however, and conditions were sometimes not what the workers had expected. The *Hampshire Chronicle* and other newspapers routinely published notices from employers offering rewards for farm servants who had absconded.

The farmers in and around Chawton who raised livestock and grew crops would have been the main employers of farm servants, as Edward Knight had little need of them. Nor did he keep household servants at Chawton. When he and his family visited the Great House, many of his household and personal servants from Godmersham—butler, cook, housekeeper, valet, footmen, maids, and so on—accompanied the family. Mrs. Austen counted 19 servants during the Knights' 1820 visit to Chawton.

Plowmen, shepherds and cowherds, dairy maids, stable-hands, carters and other such workers could find themselves working on anything from a small farm to a large estate, but there was an additional class of estate servants with no parallel on farms. These included such workers as gamekeepers, woodmen, gardeners, lodge-keepers, and kennel-keepers. Additionally, an estate might have its own carpenter (the carpenter Christopher Jackson in *Mansfield Park* seems to belong to the estate, since his labor in building theatre sets involves no extra expense). An estate-owner with coaching, hunting, and racing horses would employ more numerous and more skilled workers in the stables than a farmer would have need for—although, as Jane Austen's Mr. Bennet and Mr. Knightley show, many estate-owners did without extensive (and expensive) equine operations.

At Chawton, one essential employee at all times was the estate woodman (Knight actually employed three woodmen in Hampshire, one each at Chawton, Shalden, and Steventon). The woodman, like the gamekeeper, was in charge of managing and protecting an estate's resources. He oversaw the preparation of tree seedlings in the nursery, planting, the cutting of timber and underwood, the chopping and bundling of wood for sale, and ditching and hedging in the woodlands. The woodman showed standing timber to prospective purchasers and sold wood on behalf of his employer, earning a commission on such sales.[26] Woodmen were often hired from the ranks of agricultural laborers, but, during the years when the Great House was rented

---

[26] *In Jane Austen's letters, there is a brief reference to Cassandra providing "tapes" for Edward Knight until he bought a patent timber-measure. An important task among sellers of wood was measuring trees and calculating their volume. Many specialized devices were invented to aid in doing this, including devices with metal parts to pass under trees lying on the ground, and measuring tapes that would show a tree's diameter as well as its circumference. With three semi-literate woodmen operating in different villages, Knight may have relied on Cassandra (who seems to have been his liaison and assistant on several business matters) to procure tapes for his workers to facilitate and standardize their tree measurements.*

out to John-Charles Middleton (who as a tenant was not permitted to cut any of the trees on the estate), Knight selected as his Chawton woodman John Bunce, a dealer who often had bought wood from the Chawton estate to sell on at retail.

Additional estate servants came on board after Middleton moved out. The most important of these was the gamekeeper, William Triggs, who arrived in 1813. In addition to discouraging poachers and preserving game for the pleasure of the gentry, Triggs was a general estate factotum.

Another prestigious post was that of gardener. George Turner began his association with Knight by renting a nursery from him, most likely to cultivate plants that he sold to customers around Chawton. In 1813, he did work to improve the Chawton House gardens, and soon after began to collect a salary as the estate's gardener. This arrangement did not last long, however, as in the middle of 1814, he found a new job—"something in the Cow Line, near Rumsey" wrote Jane Austen sniffily—and went away, to everyone's relief. He was succeeded by William Pullinger, who started out working for Knight, probably only part-time, at a salary of £20 per year. By 1825, he was earning £40 annually. He held the post for many years and was succeeded by his son.

The Pullingers' history illustrates the differences in condition between a day-laborer, usually struggling to make ends meet, and an estate servant, who earned a good salary, came into contact with his employer and members of the family, and enjoyed some leisure time. Just as *Northanger Abbey*'s General Tilney "loved a garden," fussed over his pinery and glass-houses, and personally oversaw the creation of a garden at his son's house at Woodston, so Edward Knight took great interest in planning his new kitchen-garden and selecting its fruit trees and other plants. No doubt he and William Pullinger had many talks together. In the 1820s, Pullinger took up growing cucumbers, which he showed off at "cucumber feasts" around the region, sometimes gaining a prize and the satisfaction of seeing his name in the newspaper.

Planting plan for part of the Chawton Great House kitchen garden, in Edward Knight's hand.

John Browning was hired in 1813 as "yard man," and his wife became the "dairy woman." Cattle were not raised at the Great House for commercial purposes, but evidently one or two cows were kept when the house was occupied for any considerable time. Together, the Brownings probably kept an eye on the house when it was vacant and did anything that needed doing inside or outside. It is unclear where the Brownings and the Pullingers lived; William Triggs appears at times on lists of Edward Knight's rent-payers, but the Pullingers and Brownings do not. There were rooms over the stables and outbuildings near the Great House where they could have resided, and it makes sense, especially, that the dairy woman would live close to the cow and the gardener close to the garden. Edward Knight rented a cottage and garden located between the Great House and the rectory where some of his estate servants might have lived for a time, but in 1817 he bought the land and had the cottage pulled down (possibly to improve the view from the Great House).

❧ A Trusted Employee: William Triggs

Edward Knight and his children lived at Chawton Great House for five months in 1813, and, as he decided at that time to keep the house available for family use rather than rent it out, he decided to employ a gamekeeper. His sons were sport-obsessed, and his brothers also enjoyed the opportunity of shooting when they visited Godmersham or Chawton. The mass slaughter of grouse or pheasant by stationary hunters did not occur at Chawton at this time; rather, hunters went out on foot with dogs and pursued whatever game offered, or hunted foxes from horseback.

William Triggs came to Chawton from nearby Privett in the fall of 1813, collecting his first wages that Christmas. A gamekeeper's primary responsibility was to maintain the stock of birds and other game for the squire and his guests to shoot. He deterred poaching and made sure that agricultural workers' activities did not disturb nests. At Chawton, Triggs no doubt also kept an eye out for pigs and other farm animals foraging in the woods, where they might eat or disturb tree seedlings. There is no record of how many poachers Triggs warned off the land, but the accounts book bears witness to two who were formally prosecuted. In 1819, Knight's steward paid £2.4.6 to a constable who conveyed two poachers, Croucher and Stiles, to jail.

It was costly to employ a gamekeeper. Knight paid Triggs £52 a year, nearly half the sum Knight's steward received. Salary aside, the gamekeeper's certificate or license had to be purchased and renewed, meat had to be bought for his dogs, and powder and shot for his gun. He may have had a horse; Triggs bought a horse with estate funds, but whether it was for use by visiting sportsmen, by Triggs himself, or in the hayfields or woods is unclear. Similarly, £9 was paid from estate funds in 1817 to settle a charge of assault laid against Triggs after an altercation with one William Brambley, but whether their encounter was in the line of the gamekeeper's duty, we will likely never know.

Gamekeepers were, by the nature of their job, in a difficult position. Rather like governesses, who fit in neither with the family nor the servants, gamekeepers typically belonged to the laboring class but were paid to uphold the squire's sporting interests against the villagers' attempts to secure an illicit addition to their dinners. The gamekeeper's clothes were a cut above a laborer's; Jane Austen wrote about Triggs's green keeper's coat, and the estate accounts book shows that his hat cost a guinea.

In 1817, Jane wrote that "Triggs is as beautiful & condescending as ever, & was so good as to dine with us today." Her description suggests that Triggs thought rather highly of himself, but his dinner with the Austen ladies could not have been entirely comfortable for him, with Jane trying to coax conversation out of him about village goings-on and, just possibly, entertaining herself at his expense as Mr. Bennet does with Mr. Collins. In another letter, she sends her love to all, "including Triggs"; he must have been the subject of jokes within the family.

At Chawton, Triggs carried out a number of additional, unrelated functions. He managed mowing and hay-making each summer—he paid the workers who brought in the hay and the thatcher who thatched the hayrick, and he sold the hay, pocketing a commission on the sale. He oversaw a large trenching job in 1818, possibly for the new kitchen-garden, and was reimbursed for the wages he paid the laborers. These transactions show that Triggs was trusted with important work and large sums of money. He also had to lend a hand with less exalted tasks: one of Jane Austen's letters preserves a comical portrait of Triggs and Browning (the Great House yard man) running down the street, loaded down with bird-cages and luggage, to meet the coach that was to carry Mrs. Driver, the housekeeper, back to Godmersham.

Triggs and his wife Mary had seven children. Their daughter Ann grew up to be the housekeeper at an estate in West Tisted, Hampshire. Another daughter, Jane, moved to Godmersham, where she married, raised a family, and died; it seems likely that she made such a move to work on the Godmersham estate. William Triggs's son George, and then his grandson Walter, succeeded him as Knight's gamekeepers at Chawton. Triggs's eldest son and namesake shattered this picture of respectability and symbiosis with the country-house class, however. The younger William was jailed in 1832 for stealing "one fowl and a goose" at Chawton and was found guilty at the quarter sessions in 1833. He was confined on a prison ship in the harbor at Portsmouth before being transported to Australia, where he died in the hospital a few weeks after the end of the four-month voyage.

Day-Laborers

As the land Edward Knight kept in hand in Hampshire was not intensively farmed, the work in his woods and fields was done by day-laborers. They worked only when there was work to be done and received pay only when they worked. They did not receive housing on the estate, instead renting cottages or tenements in the village. They, and not their employers, were responsible for finding enough work to sustain themselves and their families. If they had no work or encountered other misfortunes, they had to seek assistance from the parish Overseers of the Poor.

Man carrying a faggot, by George Chinnery, ca 1799.

The laborers who appear most consistently in the 1808-1819 accounts are James Mersh, Abraham Knight, and William Trimmer (not to be confused with Robert Trimmer, Edward Knight's agent). All three men, and indeed all the Chawton day-laborers for whom pay receipts have been found, signed with an "X" on work vouchers, prepared by the agent's clerks, when they collected their pay.[27] Nonetheless, they would have had specialized skills and a strong familiarity with the terrain. Most would have begun work as children, working alongside their fathers—the words "and boy" often appear next to a laborer's name on work vouchers. The men earned a standard £0.2.0 per day (with a bit more for some jobs), and the boys, £0.0.6. While the wages Knight paid were good for agricultural work in southern England at the time, the day-laborers' challenge was to obtain enough work to sustain a family. Ten shillings per week was estimated to be the minimum level at which a family could be self-sustaining.

Day-laborers on the Chawton estate spent most of their time working in the woodlands. They prepared seedlings in the tree nursery and planted them in the woods, cut underwood and timber, and stripped bark from felled trees. The estate steward would engage the local sawyer, Robert Grover, to carry out the specialized job of sawing logs into building-timber, while the laborers did the less-skilled work of chopping wood to make faggots and bavins for sale as fuel. Another important task was making and repairing hedges, which bordered the various fields and copses and kept livestock from neighboring farms from wandering into the woods and eating the tender young plants. In addition to these activities, the laborers would be assigned to do anything that

---

[27] *They may have been able to read, however: some "dame schools" taught reading but not writing.*

needed doing—including working in Mrs. Austen's garden and cleaning the waste pool that served her cottage.

Women seldom participated in the woodland work that that made up the bulk of laborers' activity on Edward Knight's property. An exception is found in the vouchers of William Woods of Shalden, who claimed payment for work done by "self & girl." The Woods girl helped with planting, trimming along the roadways, cleaning up windfalls, and cutting wood in the Shalden underwoods and coppices. On one occasion, she and an unnamed woman were paid for "cleaning young plants"; the woman received £0.0.8 per day, the girl £0.0.6.[28]

In December 1808, a note in the Chawton estate accounts book states that £4.15.0 was paid to "Farmer Spencer for work by his Team [i.e., team of horses] in carrying stones to roads in woods & for picking the stones." Picking the stones from the fields was actually done by Sarah Trimmer and Olive Knight, the wives of William Trimmer and Abraham Knight. The two women collected 50 loads of stones, which over the

Haymakers, undated study by Robert Hills.

course of three days were moved to the roads by teams of seven to ten horses and set in place by men. For their part of the work—the most backbreaking part, as digging out and lifting up stones would be harder than unloading them—each woman took home £0.12.5 for the job.

In certain English counties, poor women were encouraged to engage in agricultural work for wages. The Sussex Agricultural Society gave prizes to women who kept themselves employed on the land for the largest number of days in a year (the winner, a widow, worked for 198 days). In Hampshire, however, too many male laborers were unemployed, so women's opportunities

---

[28] *This was fairly standard for women: in 1813 survey of agricultural practices in Hampshire reported that the average wage of female workers during harvest was £0.0.8 per day.*

were more limited. They performed low-paying tasks, such as stonepicking and weeding, and seasonal work, such as haymaking and hop-harvesting. Beginning in 1813, Edward Knight gave the responsibility for haymaking to William Triggs and reimbursed him for the wages he had distributed to unnamed workers, most likely women from the village. Hops were not grown on Knight's lands-in-hand in the first decades of the 19th century, but, looking forward about a century, entries for "Chawton Women" and "Farringdon Women" appear in the early 20th-century wage accounts for the hop harvests. In 1908, 61 women and 12 men brought in the crop.

In the early 19th century, many people tried to address rural poverty from both philosophical and practical perspectives. One approach taken by agricultural societies, including those in Hampshire and Kent in which Edward Knight and his son were active, was to provide monetary incentives for poor people who kept themselves employed and avoided seeking parish relief. It was something of an endurance contest, as the societies recognized those with the largest families and greatest hardships who managed to survive with the least help. Chawton villagers sometimes won these awards. In 1802, three Chawton laborers, Thomas Rout, John Ewens, and Thomas Smith, were awarded £1.1.0 each. In 1819, the Hampshire Agricultural Society awarded "£3 to William Garnett, of Chawton, labourer, he having had 18 children, of whom ten are alive, and five at home, whom he has supported with little parish relief, and bearing a most exemplary character."

❧ From Day-Laborer to Estate Servant: Abraham Knight

Between 1679 and 1852, all of the Knights who owned the Chawton estate assumed the Knight surname as a condition of inheriting the property. There were, however, many other Knights in the village of Chawton and the surrounding area who were born to that name—and to a humbler rank in society. One such was Abraham Knight, who for several decades lived with his wife and children in one half of a small brick cottage near the Chawton House gate and the Church of St. Nicholas.[29] Abraham Knight and the other occupant—laborer William Trimmer until 1811, and William Carter thereafter—rented their property from Ann Oliver, a widow living in Alton.

Abraham Knight, his wife Olive, and their children (six of whom survived infancy) were poor enough to be among those who received money when the churchwardens distributed charitable gifts in 1791, and on several occasions in 1804, Abraham appealed for help from the Overseers of the Poor. He needed help less frequently thereafter, and over time, he gained stability and perhaps a small measure of prosperity.

---

[29] The two halves of the cottage were later combined and are now known as Orchard Cottage.

Abraham Knight performed the full range of work in the woods and tree nursery and did the occasional odd job. In 1815, he secured a position as the Chawton woodman. From that point, he received a salary of £5.5.0 a year and a small commission on sales of wood. He continued to collect day-labor pay as well, and would have been well-positioned to take on as much of the available work himself as he wanted. Among his duties as woodman was showing standing timber to prospective purchasers. Although he was unable to write, he must have been able to use maps and measuring tools and to keep records in some form.

In 1825, after Ann Oliver's death, her sons sold her cottage. The auction advertisement gives some insight into the conditions in which Abraham Knight and his family lived. They and their co-tenant shared a half-acre of land containing a garden and orchard, produce from which would have helped feed the family. Edward Knight purchased the cottage and its interior fixtures (an oak dresser top, two shelves, a bacon rack, and shelves fitted in the pantry) from the Olivers, adding to his property holdings in the village while ensuring that Abraham Knight and his family could stay in their home. From this point, Abraham appears in Edward Knight's rent lists, paying £5 a year.

Although Abraham Knight left no will or personal papers, we have some idea of how he spent his leisure time and contributed to the community. In the 1830s, records show that Edward Knight's annual gift of £1.1.0 to the bell-ringers at St. Nicholas church was paid to Abraham Knight, who must have been a bell-ringer, and quite possibly the Tower Captain (lead ringer). His cottage neighbor, William Carter, played the bassoon in church.

Abraham Knight lived to the age of 84, his wife Olive to 85. They were buried in Chawton churchyard and had a headstone, which was not usual among the poor—another indication that they achieved, at least in their later years, a degree of comfort and stability.

☙ A Laboring Family in Persistent Poverty: James Mersh and Family

Like Abraham Knight, day-laborer James Mersh made and repaired hedges, planted trees, did coppicing and tree-cutting, and worked in the tree nursery, tending seedlings for later planting in the woods. In 1809, a year in which he did some work at Mrs. Austen's cottage as well as working in the woods, his earnings from Edward Knight amounted to £9.8.4 for the year.

Mersh often brought one of his sons to work alongside him. No doubt this was how his son William, who as an adult appears on the records of workers under his own name, acquired his skills. One winter, James and one of his sons, working together, dug holes and planted 950 seedlings over 16 days, taking home a combined payment of £2.0.0 for the job.

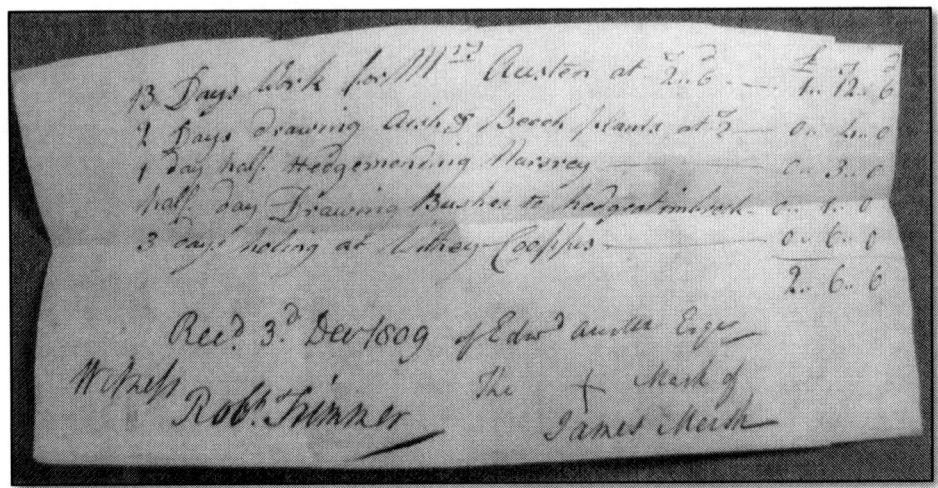

James Mersh's voucher for working at Mrs. Austen's, preparing ash and beech seedlings, mending hedges, and working in Withy Coppice.

When he was not needed on the Knight estate, Mersh probably sought work from the farmers in the area. One of his sons is known to have worked for a Chawton farmer, and probably the others did, too, to help make ends meet. At times, the family's united efforts weren't enough and their only option was to seek parish assistance. In 1804, James Mersh appealed to the Overseers of the Poor five times within six months, receiving a total of £0.19.0 in cash and a further £0.5.0 for shoes. In other years he sought only occasional assistance, until the winter of 1807-1808, when he suffered an injury to his arm. The overseers recorded him "Lying Still" for 7 weeks, during which time they granted £3.15.0 in aid and paid £0.1.0 for "Oyle" for his arm. The winter was the busiest time of year for both woodcutting and planting, so it is probable that he had an accident at work.

The family seems to have moved around quite a bit. In 1814, James Mersh first appeared as a tenant of Edward Knight's, paying £4 in rent that year. The next two years, he paid only £3; Knight may have reduced his rent or Mersh may have moved to a cheaper cottage. He then disappears from Knight's list of tenants and appears to have moved to a property owned by William Andrews. This was a hopkiln that had been converted into five tenements rented to poor villagers (now Park View Cottages). In 1818 and 1819, he rented a garden from Edward Knight but was unable to pay on time; the arrears list shows that his son also held a garden plot. In Kent, Edward Knight was one of several landowners who organized a "Labourer's Friend Society" with the object of enabling agricultural laborers to cultivate allotment gardens, and he made small plots on his estate available at nominal rents for that purpose. The garden plots at Chawton rented to Mersh and his son may have been an informal example of the same idea.

James and his wife Maria (née Browning) were parents of 11 children. One of those children has been remembered for an incident alluded to in Jane Austen's letters. In 1814, Stephen Mersh, who was about 18, was stabbed by 11-year-old James Baigen. The *Salisbury and Winchester Journal* gives the detail that Stephen Mersh (incorrectly named as Nash) was employed by Baigen's father, "an opulent farmer." In those days, the cost of prosecutions had to be paid by the victims, something the Mersh family clearly could never have afforded. The Chawton estate accounts show that Edward Knight paid £9.0.0 toward the costs of "prosecution of Baigen for cutting & stabbing Stephen Mersh."[30] The fact that there was a collection for this purpose hints at a level of community outrage about this crime. Nonetheless, the Baigen boy was acquitted. Edward Knight interested himself in the case to the extent of obtaining legal advice about the likelihood of success of a second prosecution. The case was not retried, but the incident is notable for Knight's involvement, and for the fact that his donation to the prosecution costs was nearly as much as Stephen's father earned from the estate in an entire year. Stephen survived the knife attack and lived to the age of 80.

Mersh's daughter Elizabeth experienced another kind of misfortune, this one all too common. In 1811, at the age of 19, she gave birth to an illegitimate child, whom she named George. The parish paid £1.0.0 for the costs of her lying-in, and £0.12.0 to bury her baby a short time later. They also paid £0.9.11 for "Liz" to lodge in the Dedman household for several months before the birth. It may be that she had been living elsewhere as a domestic servant and had had to return home when she became pregnant, but found her parents' home too full with other children when she returned.[31]

Farmers and Other Tenants

While Edward Knight was socially and financially the head of the Chawton community, farmers were its beating heart. It was yeoman farmers and tenant farmers (i.e., those who owned their own land and those who rented land, respectively) who gave employment to the village's plowmen, shepherds, and other farm workers. Farmers supported the community by paying rates, and they played important roles in parochial government. An assessment made in 1790 determined that three-quarters of the agricultural land in Britain was cultivated by tenant farmers, not landowners.

---

[30] *Other writers have suggested that Knight intervened on behalf of Baigen, but the payment in support of the prosecution shows that this was not the case.*
[31] *In 1876, the Hampshire Agricultural Society gave the premium for a deserving "single woman or widow above 56 years of age" employed in agriculture to Elizabeth Marsh, who worked for Mr. Holt of Chawton. The Mersh name was often spelled Marsh or Mearsh, but I have not been able to determine whether this was the same Elizabeth, or perhaps a relative.*

Farmers participated in community affairs, and some claimed the right to speak on national affairs as well. By attending the parish vestry meeting, which was essentially a local council meeting chaired by the rector but with responsibility for secular matters, Chawton's farmers took part in setting the rates to be charged for aid to the poor, the maintenance and operation of the church, and repairs to the parish's 9½ miles of roads. By serving as churchwardens (a post with as many secular responsibilities as ecclesiastical ones) and Overseers of the Poor, the farmers directly controlled how the proceeds of the rates were spent. The churchwardens' account book contains payments for repairs to and cleaning of the church; purchases of communion bread and wine; bounties paid to parishioners for killing foxes and sparrows, considered vermin; and payments to innkeepers who hosted the meetings where the churchwardens and select citizens discussed the issues of the day.

Farmers did not always share the views of their landlords. For example, in 1814, Hampshire justices of the peace, all owners of large property (including William Prowting, Edward Woolls, Harris Bigg-Wither, and William Portal, all of whom are mentioned in various contexts in Jane Austen's letters) decided that an asylum for insane paupers should be built, with funds to come from county rates. A group of tenant farmers then gathered at a Winchester

HOPS for SALE to BREWERS and DEALERS
Wholesale only.

RICHARD EVAMY begs to inform his friends in general that he has for Sale a Quantity of the very best FARNHAM and COUNTRY HOPS, of the most favorite plantations of Farnham, Bentley, Binsted, Froyle, Alton, Chawton, Shaldon, &c. which will be sold well worth the attention of Brewers in the West of England, on terms equal in price to the best Kent Hops in the London market. The Hops consist chiefly of the best quality, and will therefore be found equal to any grown in England, R.E. therefore presumes to recommend them to his friends.

Advertisement in Salisbury & Winchester Journal, *March 7, 1808. Some of Knight's tenants grew hops and may have sold to dealers like this one. Top: hop-wagon, sketch by Robert Hills.*

public house to discuss the proposal and decided to oppose it, partly on the grounds that they as "occupiers of land" paid a disproportionate share of the rates already. On the committee appointed to prepare a petition were Knight's tenant at Colemore Farm, Samuel Smith, and one of the Digweed brothers—most likely Harry, who farmed Knight land in Chawton.

One forum where landowners, tenant farmers, and, to a lesser extent, farm servants met on common ground was the agricultural society. One of the earliest of these was formed at Odiham in 1785, with Jane Austen's father among its subscribers. In 1811, the Hampshire Agricultural Society was established, with Harry Digweed as a founding member. Gentlemen of property donated silver cups and special prizes for the best farms and livestock, and members' annual subscription fees paid for other premiums. Farmers brought their plowmen to compete in plowing matches, vied to see whose shepherd could raise the most lambs, and showed off their best horses, sheep, and cattle. The agricultural society encouraged innovation and improvement, enabling farmers to assess the advantages of particular cross-breeds and to examine new machinery for threshing and planting. Edward Knight and later his eldest son, some of their tenant farmers, and laborers from Chawton are all mentioned in reports of the society's activities.

During the early years of the 19th century, "opulent" was a favored adjective used by newspapers to describe prosperous farmers, and cartoonists and social critics drew attention to farm families' rising style of living. Robert Martin in *Emma* exemplifies the progressive, successful farmer: he is attentive to the agricultural reports and well-regarded by the squire; his family enjoys their two parlors and large summer-house and looks forward to increasing their staff of

Farmer Giles and His Wife Showing off their Daughter Betty to the Neighbors, upon her Return from School, by James Gillray, 1809. Farmers who adopted the habits of the gentry were widely criticized.

indoor servants. Robert Martin's sisters attend Mrs. Goddard's school, another sign of upward mobility.

The early 19th century was a period of change in agricultural practices and instability in both commodity markets and the national currency. The first years of the century were very good for farmers as crop prices were high, and many farmers tried to cultivate as much land as they could, turning pastures into arable land and renting multiple farms. In 1802, the House of Commons expressed concern about "too considerable consolidation, and consequent enlargement of farms" in the country—a trend that was visible in Chawton and the surrounding areas. While this expansion was good for the farmers in question, it decreased the number of agricultural workers who were employed and changed the character of communities.

An 1804 print titled "The Watchful Farmer" gives another view of class tensions, with the gentlemanlike farmer stirring a lazy laborer into action.

English farmers' prosperity did not last. When grain prices were high, many had signed leases at high rents and had invested in new equipment, financed by debt. When grain prices fell precipitously at the end of the war, many farmers were unable to meet their financial commitments. Rising poor rates hit farmers hard, as increasing numbers of laborers were turned off the land by cash-strapped employers and soldiers and sailors returned from war, seeking parochial relief in growing numbers.

Edward Knight's tenant farmers were a diverse group, occupying different amounts of land and bringing varying amounts of capital to their enterprises. Their ability to withstand economic challenges varied, too. Some, like the Langrish family at Neatham Manor Farm and the Digweeds at Steventon Manor Farm, enjoyed prominence and stability, keeping their leased land in the family for several generations. The Spencers, who had held Old Park Farm in Chawton since at least 1773, farmed on a more modest scale. Thomas Spencer missed several rent payments in 1816 and 1817 but did not go under. Others were not so lucky. Robert Hall's disappearance from Steventon has already been mentioned, and Harry Digweed's dissolution is discussed later in this section. Mary Woolveridge, who held Upper Neatham Mill and 25 acres, and who co-invested with Knight in improvements to the mill between 1811 and 1814, was apparently unable to cope with the increased rent during the economic downturn; her affairs were put in the hands of trustees, and all her belongings were auctioned for the benefit of creditors in 1817.

Knight generally had about 14 tenants of farms or other large properties during this period. Six of those tenants, or their family members, held the same property over the entire 1808-1819 period; five (William Francis Digweed, the Langrishes, the Spencers, the family of Richard Andrews of Wivelrod Farm in Bentworth, and Bridger Bradley of Anstey Mill Farm near Neatham), were still in place when Knight's agent made a list of tenants in 1827.[32]

Jane Austen was comfortable around farmers, having grown up witnessing her father's enthusiasm for raising pigs and sheep and his endeavors to turn a profit from his land in Steventon. Nonetheless, her fictional farmers and farm-workers are seen mostly in passing. In *Mansfield Park*, for example, the farmers are busy with the harvest and not at all deferential to a young lady's desire for them to deliver her harp. In the beginning of *Sanditon*, Charlotte Heywood's father is out in the fields, directing his workers in cutting hay.

✺ Farmers and Community Leaders: William and Harry Digweed

Hugh and Ruth Digweed's five sons were contemporaries of George Austen's children, growing up alongside them in Steventon. Jane Austen knew the second son, Harry, well enough to write of him flippantly as "my dear Harry" in one of her early letters, and for several years she kept up a running joke that the third son, James, was in love with Cassandra.

Hugh Digweed owned farmland elsewhere in Hampshire, but by basing himself on rented land in Steventon he had control of over 1,300 acres, almost all the farmland in the parish, and could raise his family in the remains of a substantial Tudor manor house. When Hugh died in 1791, his sons Harry and William-Francis (whom Jane Austen referred to as William) became joint tenants of Steventon Manor Farm. A 1794 fire insurance inventory of the principal farm buildings on the land held by the Digweeds suggests the scale of their farming operation. There are four large barns, three of which are designated for particular crops, and additional special-purpose structures.

---

[32] *Some of the turnover is the result of deaths. For example, New Park Farm in Chawton left the Andrews family's tenancy in 1817 as a result of John Andrews' death.*

Buildings on Knight-Owned Farms in Steventon Rented by the Digweeds

Two stables, brick built and tile-roofed £50

Dog kennel containing one floor and
six bays, thatched £56

Long barn, containing two floors and
ten bays, timber built and thatched £96

Oat barn, timber built and thatched,
two floors and twelve bays £112

Granary, timber built and thatched £50

Wheat barn containing one floor and
three bays, timber built and thatched £32

Barley barn, containing two floors and
eight bays, timber built and thatched £80

Carthouse and fodder house adjoining,
timber built and thatched £50

Excerpt from insurance valuation, 1794

Harry moved away from Steventon in 1809, and William continued on as sole proprietor of the farm. William never married but, as Steventon's major land-holder and a close ally of Edward Knight, took on something of a paternal role in the community. Caroline Austen (daughter of James Austen, rector of Steventon) wrote of a dinner given in Digweed's barn to "all the poor of the parish" in honor of the King's birthday, and one of her brother's school-friends, while visiting Steventon in 1813, described the harvest festivities sponsored by William Digweed: donkey-races, sack-races, wheelbarrow-races, and so on, all with prizes. William received and put to use the donations that Knight provided to support a school in Steventon. William was a frequent guest at James Austen's table at Steventon rectory, and after James's death, William performed an important service for the remaining Austen siblings by overseeing the care of their disabled brother George, who spent most of his life with a family in Monk Sherborne. William paid George's caretaker £15 each quarter and supplied the money for anything additional that George needed (all later reimbursed by Edward Knight).

When Harry left Steventon, it was to take up the lease of the 300-acre Pound Farm in Chawton, employing a bailiff to help manage it. Harry did not live at the farm, but rather rented a smart house on Lenten Street in Alton where, for £35 per year, he and his young family had the use of two good parlors, stabling for two horses, and an excellent garden. In 1811, Harry expanded his farming operations by renting Chawton Manor Farm, gaining another 200 acres. He moved his family to the house at Manor Farm (adjacent to Chawton Great House), which they furnished with such fashionable items as a Grecian couch and mahogany Trafalgar chairs. His wife (née Jane Terry) had a small pony chaise and, like the Austen ladies, "a useful donkey" with which to make visits and travel to Alton. She was from a gentry family, and from one of her Terry relations Harry received a legacy of £1,000 in 1816.

William and Harry showed an interest in agricultural improvements and made a name for themselves as knowledgeable farmers. In 1801, the *Reading Mercury* advertised "Swedish turnip seed, the growth of Mr. Digweed, of Steventon, and warranted by him." Turnips had recently been recognized for their ability to improve the quality of the soil, in addition to being feed for livestock. At some time before 1813, William had a grain threshing mill built in a barn at Steventon Manor Farm. Agricultural journals described this innovation, giving copious details about its construction, operation, and William's expected return on investment (his £250 outlay was anticipated to be recovered within 10 years). Harry sometimes judged livestock and sheep-shearing at the Hampshire Agricultural Society's gatherings. His farming stock was extensive. He raised a large flock of "real bred South Down sheep... very superior" and kept Alderney cows and 16 cart horses. He principally grew wheat, but may have had a hop garden as well, as hop poles and other equipment were among the items auctioned when he left off farming.

Harry took his turns as churchwarden, overseer, and tax collector in Chawton, but he had wider interests, seeking roles that placed him in company with the gentry. Along with his brother William, James Austen, and an array of Hampshire peers and politicians, Harry signed an 1805 petition opposing a Parliamentary resolution of thanks to the Earl of St. Vincent, who had been accused of corruption while First Lord of the Admiralty. Harry belonged to the Society for the Promotion of Christian Knowledge and served on one of its committees. In 1819, he was part of the management committee (along with Frank Austen, Charles Trimmer, John Papillon, and others) of the Provident Institution Savings Bank in Alton, a philanthropic endeavor designed to encourage the poor to save, for which Edward Knight was a trustee.

The Hampshire Agricultural Society awarded Harry a special honorary premium for a "well-cultivated farm" in 1821. This may have been an attempt by his friends to encourage or console him, because by then Harry, despite encouraging the poor to practice thrift, was himself in financial trouble. In 1822, all his household and farm assets were sold at auction. He and his family, apparently fleeing creditors, took refuge in Brussels, Belgium, a city that a guidebook of the period recommended as ideally adapted to "persons going abroad with slender purses." A few years later, he wrote a letter to a prominent Hampshire politician in the hopes of getting one of his sons, whom he could not afford to keep at Oxford, set up in the Army without purchasing a commission. Harry wrote that he had had to "save my disposable property from mortgage claimants in England" and that his £2,000, which he had converted to Dutch securities upon his arrival in Brussels, had fallen to half its value as a consequence of the Belgian revolution. Harry and his family moved to Paris, where he died in 1848, his wife in 1860.

William Digweed continued to farm in Steventon until his death in 1863. A nephew took his place and continued until 1877, outlasting the Knights, who sold their land in Steventon in 1855.

❧ Yeoman and Tenant: John Andrews

The three John Andrews, grandfather, father, and son, exemplified solid yeoman farmer stock, prosperous yet unpretentious. Their names are not found on political petitions and lists of committees printed in the newspapers, but they accumulated a significant amount of property and passed it to a large number of descendants.

The first John Andrews (who died in 1774) leased New Park Farm in Chawton in the 1750s and some years later took on Common Farm too, approximately 600 acres in all. The family was originally from Medstead, west of Chawton. They maintained strong ties in their native village while accumulating property around the region. By the time the second John Andrews died in 1811 (leaving £100 to each of ten grandchildren), he owned farmland and houses in Medstead, as well as property in Farringdon, a house in Ropley, and another in Alton. He also held land by copyhold (i.e., manorial tenancy) in Nettlebed and Old Alresford. He retired in 1809 to a house on Cross and Pillory Lane in Alton, leaving his son to manage the farms.

His eldest son, the third John Andrews, inherited the lease to New Park Farm and Common Farm. He also leased the tithes for these properties from the rector, a transaction that enabled him to keep all the produce of the farms in exchange for a fixed fee. The 1816 table of crops grown at New Park Farm shows the nature of farming at the time: land was divided into many fields of different sizes, where a variety of crops were raised (with a different planting in each field each year). Fields were periodically left uncultivated (layn) for up to two years to improve the soil.

John Andrews was financially comfortable and linked by marriage to many of the established farming families in the area, but he and his family apparently did not aspire to the sort of social prominence that the Digweeds pursued. Andrews held a certificate to shoot game—not a deputation given by the Lord of the Manor such as Harry Digweed and John Langrish held, but rather a general certificate that cost more and gave fewer privileges.

Fanny Knight recorded in her diary in 1809 that she walked with her aunts Jane and Cassandra to New Park Farm but does not mention meeting anyone there. In 1815, Jane wrote to Cassandra, "Poor Farmer Andrews! I am so sorry

List of crops at New Park Farm, 1816

New Park Farm Fields	Size (Acres, Rods, Perches)	Use
Upper Pond Close	17.0.20	Oats with grass seeds
Hither Pond Close	15.2.10	Turnips
Upper 12 Acres	12.1.0	Sainfoin, 1 year
Hither 12 Acres	11.3.10	Green wheat
Tillings Wood	12.1.30	2 years layn
Great Brickkiln Close	20.2.30	Oats with grass seeds
Little Brickkiln Close	5.1.20	Pasture
Long Bottom	13.3.28	Green wheat
New S------	18.3.34	Wheat stubble
Home Field	12.2.12	2 years layn
Nine Acres	7.1.20	Green wheat
Hither Parke	10.0.10	Part 2 years layn, the rest peas
Seven Acres	5.2.0	2 years layn
Lower Parke	15.0.30	8 acres green wheat, rest 2 years layn
1st Sanisis	9.0.20	Barley with grass seeds
2nd Sanisis	11.0.0	Barley
3rd Sanisis	14.3.20	5 acres green wheat, rest turnips
Great Cooks Field	11.1.30	Green wheat
Little Cooks Field	4.0.10	Wheat stubble
White Down Field	33.3.23	8 acres oats, rest wheat stubble
Toleys	2.0.0	Young hops, turnips
Mounters	11.0.0	Barley with grass seeds
Keen	0.3.0	Hops
Ridgeclose	2.2.30	Barley with grass seeds
Lower Long Lands	4.2.20	Wheat stubble
Upper Long Lands	5.1.30	Old sainfoin
Reads Close	3.0.30	Turnips

for him, & sincerely wish his recovery." Despite this sympathy, there is no indication that Jane Austen was on familiar terms with any of the Andrews family. She once reported having seen Mrs. Andrews, without any indication of having spoken to her. She wrote of exchanging remarks on the hay and wheat crops with Edward Woolls, a substantial freeholder and magistrate in Farringdon, and of Miss Woolls calling at her home, but Farmer Andrews and his family were on a different rung of the social ladder. In *Emma*, many of the title character's remarks about Robert Martin are unjust, but Jane Austen may have reflected her own social conditions and attitudes in Emma Woodhouse's explanation that:

> The yeomanry are precisely the order of people with whom I feel I can have nothing to do. A degree or two lower, and a creditable appearance might interest me; I might hope to be useful to their families in some way or other. But a farmer can need none of my help, and is therefore, in one sense, as much above my notice as in every other way he is below it.

Tradesmen and Merchants

Edward Knight's steward consistently did business with a small number of skilled tradesmen who performed repairs and improvements to his properties and made the equipment needed on the estates. Most villages had their own tradesmen: the carpenters, thatchers, and other tradesmen who worked on Knight's property in Chawton lived in Chawton and Farringdon for the most part, while their counterparts four miles away in Neatham handled jobs in Neatham, and so on. One exception was John Dyer, based in Alton, who successfully conducted business over a larger area. Dyer performed a large amount of building work for Knight in Chawton, including renovations done to the former steward's cottage before Mrs. Austen, her daughters, and Martha Lloyd moved in. John Dyer, along with his sons William and George, established the beginnings of a substantial building business that lasted for more than a century. The large house they built for themselves during the Victorian period still stands in Alton today.

Some of Chawton's tradesmen were less financially stable. Carpenter Thomas Jones's daily rate for his own work was £0.2.8, not much more than agricultural day-laborers routinely received; he, alone among the village's tradesmen, could not write. William Goodchild, thatcher, received occasional aid from the Overseers of the Poor and supplemented his income by digging graves in Chawton churchyard, which suggests that his trade was much less regular and less lucrative than others. In later years, he taught the boys' class at Sunday School at his home in one of the Malthouse Cottages.

Tradesmen engaged in a more diverse range of jobs in the early 19th century than became the norm later on. Thomas Jones, carpenter, hewed timber, made gates and window frames, built packing cases, and mended doors and fences. William Gold, mason, put tile roofs on buildings as well as laying bricks. James Clinker, blacksmith, performed every type of metalwork. In 1809, he billed Knight for services that included altering casements, affixing spikes to the pigeon house, mending the fittings on Knight's coach, fixing the timber carriage, sharpening the tools used by laborers in the woods, making keys for doors at Mrs. Austen's, and producing all kinds of nails, clasps, and springs.

Dr. Munro's Carpenter at Work by William Henry Hunt, ca. 1815.

While most of the tradesmen listed above often had work of some type underway for Knight or one of his tenant farmers, Knight's steward also engaged with other craftsmen, merchants, and specialists throughout the region on a sporadic basis. Most of these additional people were called upon as needed to provide materials or perform specialized tasks related to the wood business, complementing the general labor provided by Abraham Knight, James Mersh, and other day-laborers. For example, the plants and rods for hedge-making were bought from John and Thomas Bunce, and Knight's laborers did the actual hedge-making. Specialists would sometimes be engaged to survey the woods, advise on areas to be cut, and determine the value of wood to be sold. Laborers would cut trees and bring the wood to a central point using a horse-drawn timber carriage, and then a carrier would load it onto wagons and convey it to the buyer.

Knight's steward dealt with merchants and tradesmen as a seller as well as a buyer. John and Thomas Bunce purchased faggots and brush from tree-trimming for sale around the region as hearth fuel. Thomas Eggar, an Alton tanner, purchased bark for use in tanning leather. John Dyer purchased oak timber by the load for use in his building business. Edward Andrews, who sold Knight a timber carriage in 1809, bought two mature beech trees at the same time.

ᔔ Solid Citizen: William Gold

Before Mrs. Austen and her daughters moved to the cottage in Chawton in 1809, Edward Knight decided to have the drawing-room window that faced the street blocked up and a new window created, overlooking the garden. The neat brickwork filling in the old window cavity was most likely the work of William Gold, a Chawton mason. For many years, Knight's steward engaged Gold for all kinds of masonry work, from small repairs to construction of new cottages, and Gold made a substantial amount of money from work on Knight-owned buildings. In 1812, he earned £185 for improving Butts Cottages, tenements that were let to the parish for the use of the poor. The next year, he made £177 converting a malthouse to four cottages.[33] In 1817, he built Chalkpit Cottages, also rented to the parish to house the poor, and a cottage on Chawton common, all for £94. Gold's standard rate for a day's work done by himself was £0.4.6, but he also billed for supplies and for the labor of his workers.

Gold first appears in the Chawton land tax records in 1811 as the occupier of a parcel of land owned by William Prowting, the local magistrate and second-largest landowner in Chawton. Gold and his wife Sarah were living in the village well before 1811, but may have first occupied a dwelling too

insignificant to be listed separately in the tax records. He prospered, eventually owning a two-story brick house set back from the Winchester Road, as well as now-demolished workshops and another house nearby. His 1836 will reveals that he possessed wagons, carts, and horses for his business, and that his home contained "plate, linen, china, and glass" as well as ordinary goods and utensils.

The Golds' house in Chawton, as it appears today.

For many years, William Gold served as collector of the land tax. Between 1811 and 1819, he served in this post in all but two years; often, he was paired with James Clinker, blacksmith. Gold also served for many years as an

---

[33] *These can still be seen on Chawton's main street, across from Chawton Great House.*

Overseer of the Poor, a job that required considerable administrative skill and diplomacy. The overseers collected Poor Rate payments from those with means and handled almost daily appeals from those without. The overseers had to have an understanding of the Poor Law and keep detailed accounts of all expenditures. They determined whether individuals had settlement—a legal right to claim aid from a particular parish—and they assisted, and moved along, the transient poor. They housed the neediest families in tenements owned or rented by the parish. They conducted bastardy investigations, interviewing unwed pregnant women so that the costs of raising illegitimate children could be borne by the fathers rather than by the parish. The overseers bought shoes and round frocks for needy laborers and outfitted boys and girls who were leaving the village to go into service. They arranged community support for individual needs: the Chawton overseers' accounts document instances where village women were paid at various times to wash and mend clothes for a single man, care for the ill, and shelter an unmarried pregnant girl. The overseers even paid the Poor Rate on behalf of a widow who was well-off enough to be charged £0.4.0 but too poor to pay it without hardship.

In parishes throughout the country, overseers were criticized for withholding assistance. In 1823, Chawton residents William Vast and William Mitchell (who were not themselves particularly poor, but who happened to be the Golds' near neighbors) stirred up discontent, alleging that "Gold, principal overseer, and his wife starved the poor, and put the money into their own pockets." Mitchell even circulated a gruesome story that Mrs. Gold had pushed food into the mouth of a dead pauper to make it appear he had not starved. In response, according to the *Hampshire Chronicle*, Edward Knight and members of the vestry presented Mr. and Mrs. Gold with "a very handsome Silver Cream Jug," engraved to signify their confidence in the couple's integrity and good service. Years later, in making his will, William Gold made a special mention of one prized possession: "the silver cream jug presented to me by the Parish of Chawton," which he left to his son.

The Parson

The parson[34] was an important figure in community life. In concept, the Lord of a Manor gave a clergyman a living, the job of serving the church on his land, and that clergyman was entitled to tithes, 10% of everything that grew within the parish, including crops and livestock. By the early 19th century, however, this system had become complicated: the right to select the clergyman could be sold; the right to collect tithes could be leased; and a

---

[34] *Clergymen could be rectors, vicars, or curates—but "parson" was a popularly used, all-purpose term.*

The Tythe Pig, a joke that was repeated in many forms, including prints and china ornaments. When the parson comes to collect one of ten piglets as his share of the farm's produce, the farmer and his wife press him to take their tenth child as well.

clergyman could hold multiple livings, serving all, some, or none of the churches himself.

Cartoons of the era often featured a wealthy, overfed, grasping parson as a stock character. Another stereotypical figure was the starving curate who performed the parson's religious duties but received only a fraction of his pay. Jane Austen's portrayal of the clergy varied over the course of her writing life. In *Northanger Abbey*, Henry Tilney's habit of visiting his parish only rarely, when it was made necessary by the absence of his curate or the demands of a parish meeting, passes without criticism. In *Sense and Sensibility*, Edward Ferrars expresses a preference for the church, but his acquisition of the living of Delaford is presented as a solution to his financial difficulties, rather than the accomplishment of a professional goal. In *Mansfield Park*, the differences of opinion between Edmund Bertram and Mary Crawford dramatize a debate about how a clergyman ought to live. In *Emma,* the demands of parish business are alluded to on several occasions: Mr. Elton is (if his wife is to be believed) always busy responding to inquiries from the "magistrates, and overseers, and churchwardens."

Parsons participated in local government through the vestry. They had a special responsibility for the welfare of the poor, but were usually allies of the rich, to whom they owed their livings and at whose table they often ate. Many clergymen were the younger sons of landed gentlemen, and all clergymen were gentry by virtue of their profession. In some parishes, the only genteel houses were the squire's and the parson's (this is the case at Uppercross, in *Persuasion,* before a farmhouse is "elevated" into a residence for Charles and Mary Musgrove), so it was natural that the squire and the parson would stick together.

❧ John-Rawstorne Papillon

John-Rawstorne Papillon was rector of Chawton from 1802 until his death in 1837. His father, David Papillon, was a Member of Parliament and Commissioner of Her Majesty's Excise, and owned an estate at Acrise and Lee in Kent. The Papillons were well known to the Knight family, having common relations in the Brodnaxes, and had sold the manor of Bower near Molash to them; later, David Papillon sold to Catherine Knight the house in Canterbury where she spent her final years. David Papillon's eldest son Thomas inherited his estate, and John, as the younger son, was educated for the church at Queen's College, Oxford. In 1794, Thomas Knight II appointed John to the next presentation of the living of the Church of St. Nicholas at Chawton. Papillon would have to wait until the then-current rector, John Hinton, died, and, if he chose not to accept the living, it would go instead to Henry Austen. Henry (via his brother Edward) offered John Papillon £1,200 to give up his right to the post, but Papillon did not relinquish it, and in 1802 became rector.

One of Papillon's first acts upon taking up his living was to have the parsonage house rebuilt, using some of the materials from the previous building. In his small, square new house (now overwhelmed by large additions made in the Victorian

The Chawton rectory as it appeared in the early 19th century.

period), Papillon lived with his unmarried sister, Elizabeth, who found a friend in Fanny Knight. Aside from the house, the rectory property included a one-acre garden, a coal house, a wood or straw house, a hen house, and two large barns where tithes paid in kind had been stored in former days. The glebe land comprised 5 acres of coppice and about 60 acres of fields and meadows. He kept a team of horses for working the farm, and he gained favor with Mrs. Austen by sending his team to deliver gravel and chalk to her garden at the cottage.

Although Papillon was rector of Chawton until his death, from 1816 his attention was often drawn elsewhere. He inherited the manor and estate of Lexden, near Colchester, from his godmother. Henry Austen was just then casting about for employment after the failure of his bank and other business ventures. Papillon hired Henry Austen as his curate at £52 a year, freeing himself to visit Lexden as he pleased. Henry Austen married as his second wife Papillon's niece, Eleanor Jackson, in 1820.

Papillon apparently got along well in the community. In 1815, he voluntarily reduced his tithes by 15%, providing a degree of relief to hard-pressed farmers (and, by extension, their laborers) in the parish. His sister Elizabeth made charitable visits to the poor, on at least one occasion in the company of Jane Austen. Papillon himself carried on the country custom of giving small sums of money from his own pocket to poor villagers who called at his house on St. Thomas's Day (December 21).

Other charitable causes near and far received his support: he contributed to subscriptions for various poor widows in Hampshire and for the "distressed in Germany." He served on the Alton committee of the Society for Promoting Christian Knowledge, one of the aims of which was to distribute Bibles and religious tracts among the "lower orders," as well as the Society for Promoting the Education of the Poor in the Principles of the Established Church. His sister Elizabeth supported a "female asylum" in Winchester that sheltered and found employment for poor girls. In 1819, he joined the management committee for the Provident Institution Savings Bank, designed to help the working classes establish savings, of which Edward Knight was a trustee.

Papillon was not unreservedly a champion of the lower classes, however; he was a signatory to a petition opposing a Parliamentary investigation into the massacre of protesting workers at Peterloo, near Manchester, in 1819, and he took full advantage of the 1821 enclosure of the common lands at Lexden, which enriched his estate at the expense of poorer residents of the community. Still, his influence—and the close ties among landowner, parson, and tenants—may have contributed to Chawton's stability and relative lack of social unrest. In the early 1830s, the parson in the nearby parish of Selborne, by most accounts an arrogant, unsympathetic man, was frightened by a bullet fired through his window and took to keeping a vicious dog for protection. In Selborne, Holybourne, and elsewhere, riots broke out, but Chawton remained calm.

Jane Austen teasingly wrote, "I will marry Mr. Papillon, whatever may be his reluctance or my own." He never married her, or anyone else. When he died in 1837, he left his sister a life interest in his estate and left £20 per year to support the national school in Lexden.

Others in the Community

With roughly 350 people in the parish of Chawton, there were some residents who were not direct participants in the estate economy that is documented in Edward Knight's accounts book. They included one or two genteel families, such as that of Captain Clement, and yeoman farmers, such as William Baigen. There were merchants and tradesmen, such as Edward Philmore and William Mitchell, who looked to clients other than Knight for their livelihood. There were paupers, who were beneficiaries of Knight's charity and his contribution to the poor rates. And there were widows and spinsters, including Miss Benn, whose brother, the rector of Farringdon, could not support her; Mrs. Heath, who was possibly related to John Heath, Elizabeth Knight's steward in the early 18th century; and Dame Lipscomb, a widow whose various troubles Jane Austen alluded to in her letters.

Among the widows of Chawton was Mrs. Austen, who, with her two unmarried daughters and their friend Martha Lloyd, took up residence in the former steward's cottage in July 1809. The Austen women were in a slightly perplexing situation— related to the squire yet transparently lacking the means to live in anything close to the style of the Great House—but it was not a terribly unusual one for widowed or unmarried women of their class. Wealthy widows and those who had owned property in their own right, such as Thomas Knight II's widow Catherine Knight (and the fictional Dowager Lady Dalrymple of *Persuasion*), often had independent establishments, but widows without means were lucky to be granted a rent-free cottage on a relative's estate, as Mrs. Norris in *Mansfield Park* was on the Bertram estate.

The Gothic window at Jane Austen's House Museum. Edward Knight had this window put in prior to his mother and sisters' move to the cottage, replacing a window that had overlooked the street.

Jane Austen in Chawton

The Austen women's move to Chawton came about after a deliberate search. Mrs. Austen was determined to leave Southampton, where they had lived since 1806, but she was not willing to jump at the first alternative that offered. In June 1808, Jane wrote about a Rose Hill Cottage (not otherwise identified), which was "so near suiting" their requirements; she was "almost sorry" that they were going to cross it off their list of possible homes—but she was not quite entirely sorry. They would continue to search for "something perfectly unexceptionable," perhaps in the town of Alton, with Henry Austen's help, though there was also some talk of Wye, in Kent. At the beginning of October 1808, Jane wrote that her mother "thinks much more of Alton, & really expects to move there." Eight day later, at Godmersham, Edward Knight's wife, Elizabeth, suddenly died. In the following weeks, the search for an ideal place gave way to a firm decision to move to Chawton. There are many possible reasons for this decision. Perhaps Henry failed to find anything worth considering at Alton, or Knight may have convinced his mother that it was foolish to pay rent in Alton when he could supply a house rent-free two miles away. Mrs. Austen and her daughters may have chosen an alternative that kept them at a distance from Godmersham, where they might have felt obligated to care for Knight's now motherless children more than they would like. Edward and his sister Cassandra were always close, and it is possible that, after the death of his Hampshire steward, he could see the value of having Cassandra living in the heart of Chawton, keeping an eye on things and acting informally as his representative; whether this was his intent or a fortunate side-effect, he quickly came to depend upon her practical good sense and ability to communicate his directions.

> ## "Everybody is acquainted with Chawton & speaks of it as a remarkably pretty village"
>
> Jane Austen, November 20, 1808 letter

Whatever the primary reason for the move may have been, it seems certain that looking around and considering possibilities was no longer appealing to Mrs. Austen and her daughters, and being settled came to seem more important than finding something "unexceptionable."

The cottage in Chawton, set close to a busy road, was not perfect—Anna Lefroy deemed it "not very good"—but Edward was determined to make it as close to suiting his mother as he could. His improvements to the exterior included bricking over a window that faced the road and creating a new window on the side, giving a garden view. A hedge was planted around the grounds, and within its boundaries there was room for a shrubbery walk, a small orchard, and gardens where Mrs. Austen enjoyed working. Knight sent workers to make any repairs or improvements his mother desired, and he furnished her with all the firewood needed to ensure comfort.

The kind of life Jane Austen had in Chawton was different from what she might have experienced had the party of women decided to live in Alton or a similar town. Alton had a larger population, recently built houses, and shops, among them the stationer's shop where the Alton Book Society kept its special bookshelf for members. Chawton was a country village, and despite Austen's famous remark about "3 or 4 families in a country village" being the perfect matter for a novelist, she was hard pressed to find that many congenial families, or even individuals that she desired as friends, there.

To the left of the Austens' new home was the shop of James Clinker, blacksmith, with its attendant noise and smells. Along the street by the cottage wall passed carriages conveying the well-

> "This is a delightful day in the country.... It appeared so likely to be a wet evening that I went up to the Gt. House between three and four, and dawdled away an hour very comfortably, though Edwd. was not very brisk. The air was clearer in the evening and he was better. We all five walked together into the kitchen garden and along the Gosport road, and they drank tea with us."
>
> *Jane Austen, June 13, 1814 letter*

to-do to Winchester, London, and other places, but the road was also used by farmers' carts, herders driving animals, and laborers on their way to or from work. At the time of the Austen ladies' residence, a pair of dilapidated tenements, made partly of wattle and daub and partly of brick, stood just across the pond from their home. The laborers' families who lived in them were among the Austens' nearest neighbors. One of the families was the Whites—possibly the family of John White, born in 1821, who in his old age wrote his recollections of childhood in Chawton. He naturally did not mention Jane Austen, but his memories of Cassandra suggest that he kept a curious eye on the doings of the women living across the road, and he was probably not the only one.

Altogether, the village close by the Austens' walls was far more active than the tranquil scene it presents today. Jane Austen took an interest in the comings and goings in the village, and she and her mother and sister participated in village life to varying degrees. Mrs. Austen seems to have found it a congenial setting, and she managed to stay on good terms with the Hintons and Baverstocks even when they were engaged in a legal challenge against her son. Jane's letters tell of Cassandra being visited by Abraham Knight's daughter Harriet every day for reading lessons, and of Jane's own approval of the "well behaved, healthy, large-eyed" Garnett children, to whose mother Jane brought an old shift. In general, however, Jane seems to have preferred to be an observer rather than a participant. She wrote in her letters about villagers' disputes but did not attempt to intervene, even when it looked like her friend Miss Benn might be forced out of her home. Jane may have found a necessary refuge behind the bricked-over window, the high walls enclosing the garden, and the locked back gate. She had her shrubbery walk where she could exercise and think, and sometimes she took the opportunity to avoid the village street when she went visiting by climbing over the stile that connected the Austens' garden with the Prowtings'.

Jane Austen may have had a more active social life if she had lived elsewhere, but at least at Chawton she was seldom the prisoner of the sort of "stupid parties" she had deplored many years earlier while staying in Bath. Chawton was like her childhood home in Steventon, with natural scenery and agricultural activities to observe. Residing in Chawton gave her relative freedom from social expectations, a close view of the activities and concerns of her estate-owning brother, and the time and peacefulness that enabled her to perfect her art and bring her novels to fruition.

The cottage where Jane Austen lived from 1809 until 1817, now Jane Austen's House Museum.

6. Evolution of the Chawton Estate

In managing his estate, Edward Knight made many decisions with an eye toward the future and with the intent of ensuring the prosperity of his successors. He could not predict the world events and economic changes that eroded the underpinnings of English estates in the late 19th and early 20th centuries, however. If he could look at the Knight estates, as they exist today,

Chawton House, 2013.

on a map, he would see that little remains of the vast acreage he inherited and managed with such care. If, however, he could visit Chawton House and walk around its grounds, the landscape and buildings he would see would be comfortingly familiar. One can only imagine what he, or his sister Jane, would think of Chawton House Library and the level of activity and public interest that it has brought to the stately Elizabethan mansion.

The Next Heir: Edward Knight II

Many changes to the Knight estates occurred during the tenure of Edward Knight II. Though he was only 23 when she died, Jane Austen knew her nephew well. She took pride in caring for him and his brother George for a short time after their mother died, and during that visit she made an engaging pen-portrait of a young and rather serious Edward "twisting himself about in one of our great chairs," reading *Lake of Killarney*. Some years later, she found he had become, at nineteen years of age, "a very promising and pleasing young man," more interested in field sports than she would have liked, but well-behaved and devoted to his family.

Young Edward's destiny had been clear since his birth. He would inherit the Knight property and live the life of a landed proprietor. He went to school at Winchester College and, for a time, at Oxford, then followed in his father's footsteps and visited the court in Saxony as part of his tour to the continent. From his youth, his father prepared him for his future responsibilities, taking him along on visits to Chawton when he was a schoolboy and later including him in meetings with lawyers about the Baverstock case. When he turned 21, this milestone was a community event at Godmersham, with tenants and villagers joining in the celebrations for their future squire. As a young man, he received a regular allowance of £800 per year as well as other intermittent payments or gifts.

Father and son, though sharing a name, had very different personalities. The younger Edward had two strong interests that his father did not: sport and politics. From his youth he had taken advantage of the sporting possibilities at Chawton, where he could ride and shoot over 3,000 acres. Always a keen hunter—"ever the first and foremost, always with the hounds"— he rode with the Hampshire Hunt. Cricket was also a favorite pastime: in 1824, Edward and four of his brothers took to the pitch on Selborne Common as part of a Chawton-and-Farringdon side, beating a team put together by a local baronet.

Politically, with his father well established in Kent, Edward II decided early on to make his mark in Hampshire, even before residing there full-time. In 1820, he offered himself as a candidate for Parliament but withdrew after a better known contender entered the race. He announced his withdrawal in the *Salisbury and Winchester Journal*, concluding with a statement his father, who steadfastly refused to seek a seat in Parliament, would never have made: "I wish it to be distinctly understood, that the honour of representing this County in Parliament will be ever the great object of my ambition, and I hope by a more constant residence among you than has hitherto been in my power, to prove myself worthy of your trust on some future occasion."

He embarked on a campaign to make himself better known. He joined the Hampshire Agricultural Society in 1820 (six years later, he co-founded a successor society, the East Hampshire Agricultural Society, and served as its president for four decades). In 1821, he qualified as a Deputy Lieutenant and Officer of Militia for Hampshire, based on his status as heir apparent to lands at Chawton and Farringdon. In 1823, he served as sheriff for the county, matching the £100 stipend he received for conducting the ceremonial opening of the county assizes with £100 of his own, which he spent on hospitality for the judges and fancy coats for the "javelin men" who paraded through the streets of Winchester as the cathedral bells rang. In that same year, he served as Steward of the Winchester Races, overseeing the entertainment for the genteel race-goers and contributing 25 guineas to the prize for one of the races, dubbed the "Chawton Stakes."

In late 1825, he began another run at Parliament, but not in Hampshire. This time, he tried for a seat representing Rochester in Kent, taking advantage of another candidate's surprise retirement. Again, he withdrew. His political ambition would remain unsatisfied, but he did fulfill his promise of "more constant residence" in Hampshire. Edward Knight I had planned to rent out the Great House again, but instead of finding a new tenant, he allowed his son to take up permanent residence there after Edward eloped in 1826 with Mary-Dorothea Knatchbull, his sister Fanny's stepdaughter. Mary-Dorothea's father, Sir Edward Knatchbull of Mersham Hatch, Kent, was implacably opposed to the marriage,[35] so settling in Hampshire had its advantages.

Edward Knight II in later life, from a painting by Francis Grant.

Rather than being merely an heir-in-waiting (as Jane Austen's Tom Bertram was), Edward II now had a formal role as de facto squire of Chawton. His father continued to come to Chawton to review the estate accounts with Charles Trimmer, and the younger Edward had to defer to his father on estate business, but he was able to take on in Hampshire some of the same important civic roles as his father held in Kent. Edward Knight II was a justice of the peace, and in time became the senior magistrate for Hampshire. He chaired the Chawton vestry, debating the perennial question of what to do about the poor (one solution, tried in the 1830s, was to give cash incentives to villagers willing to emigrate overseas). He contributed £200 to repairs of the church in Chawton in 1837, and another £200 to renovate the church in Farringdon. In 1852, he paid £250 to rebuild the school in Farringdon. The Hampshire Friendly Society, a laborers' mutual benefit society, received his support, as did the Society for the Propagation of the Gospel in Foreign Parts, the Alton Rifle Corps, and the Alton Mechanics' Institute. On the national level, he served as a founding director of a livestock insurance company launched in 1855.

---

[35] *The scandal of the elopement and Knatchbull's opposition seems to have dealt the death blow to Edward's political ambitions, causing him to withdraw from the Rochester race. After the initial shock, Edward's own father was more open-minded about the marriage, writing in 1830, "He is a lucky Fellow to have met with such a Companion for Life."*

Chawton Great House was a livelier place with a squire in full-time residence. Edward Knight II had seven children by his first wife, and nine by his second. To suit the needs of his family and extensive staff, he added a new servants' hall and billiard room (since demolished). The Hampshire Hunt often met on Chawton lands, and Edward became master of the hunt in 1850. He started a tradition of hosting annual festivities for tradesmen and servants at the Great House, where "the old baronial hall was again filled by the company" and "many a heart rejoiced in the bounty of the Squire."

A Time of Changes

In 1852, Edward Knight I died, leaving monetary legacies to his younger children and, as expected, all his property to his eldest son. When the *Reading Mercury* published a list of leading Hampshire landowners under the heading "The New Domesday Book" in 1876, Edward Knight II was among Hampshire's top 35 landowners, owning 5,044 acres, which brought in reported rents of £4,291. The Knight estate was not the same as it had been when his father inherited it, however. Property had been sold, concentrating the estate in Chawton and environs. The large farm at Colemore was sold in

---

... You will succeed to an ample Estate after all the Incumbrances are paid off and you will find Papers tied up with this containing my Opinion of the best mode of raising the money necessary to set you quite clear, which you may act upon in part or in the whole as may be thought most expedient. The different annuities I have directed to be paid are such as I am sure you must approve of, and I rest assured of you confirming and securing them to the several Annuitants, should a want of Assets in my personal Property render such an Act expedient. I can not too forcibly endeavor to impress on you the expediency I may say necessity of living for some years very much within your income, which whether you remain single or marry may with common Prudence easily be affected, you will by so doing be enabled to pay off many of the Charges on the Estate without materially lessening it. You will always have a Sum of Money at Command, which let your Income be what it may is a most desirable and as far as Comfort is concerned a most indispensable possession.

You had better manage your own affairs as much as you can, and have frequent settlements with any Agents you may employ. You will I trust never allow yourself to be drawn into the ruinous Expenses of a contested Election, which would probably leave you in distress'd Circumstances for the remainder of your Life and deprive you of the means of giving that occasional Assistance to your Brothers and Sisters which both Affection and Inclinations would otherwise naturally lead you to. Remember that whatever your possessions are you are accountable to God for the use you make of them.... May God assist and direct you. So prays your affectionate Father – Edwd. Knight.

Part of the letter of guidance that Edward Knight I wrote to his son in 1824

1824, and the manor of Shalden and farmland at Wivelrod (1,225 acres in all) in 1840. The Steventon property, 1,770 acres, was sold in 1855 to the Duke of Wellington. The connection to Kent was broken in 1874, when Godmersham Park was sold to an industrial magnate from Manchester.

Offsetting these sales, both the elder and younger Edward Knight bought additional property in and around Chawton when the opportunity arose, adding the land of old families, such as the Prowtings and Baigens, to the Knight estate. By the early 20th century, the Knights owned all but two houses in the village.

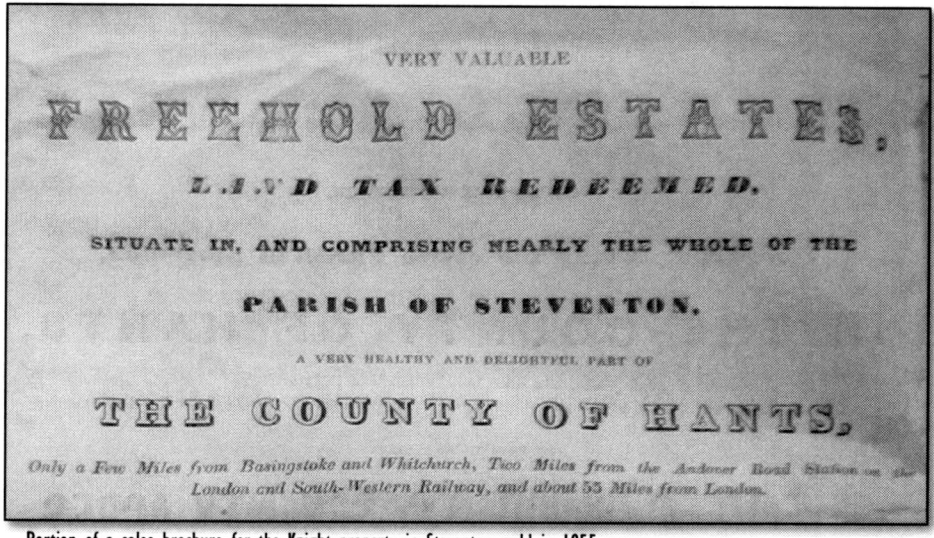

Portion of a sales brochure for the Knight property in Steventon, sold in 1855.

As outlying rental properties were sold off, the lands-in-hand at Chawton were put to increased use. Sheep were purchased for the Chawton meadows in the 1830s (there is no sign in the 1808-1819 estate accounts that Edward Knight I had kept a flock there during that period, though he did raise sheep at Godmersham). Farming activity increased and diversified. An estate wages book begun in 1907 shows payments made to more than 60 people, including brickmakers, shepherds and cowherds, dairy workers, woodmen, farm workers, threshers, sheep-shearers, hop-pickers, carters, hurdle-

Unidentified estate workers and G. Brook Knight, who helped to manage the estate in the 1930s.

makers, and thatchers. Their skills were largely the same as those practiced by Elizabeth Knight's workers two centuries earlier. Many of the surnames of the 20th century workers are familiar from the early 19th century accounts book, and some of them can be found in records dating back a further century.

Such apparent continuity and vitality were deceptive. Chawton held out longer than many places, but changes to the estate economy were already well advanced by 1900. Between 1870 and 1914, land values plummeted as foreign grain and other commodities undercut British-grown products. In 1911, Montagu George Knight, son of Edward Knight II, collaborated with William Austen-Leigh to produce *Chawton Manor and Its Owners: A Family History*. It was a well-researched and comprehensive study, but strictly backward-looking: Knight and Austen-Leigh ended their history with the death of Edward Knight II in 1879.

Death duties, introduced in 1894, and estate duty, instituted in 1914, hit the landowning class hard. During the First World War, many estates lost their labor force, and when the war ended many former estate workers sought opportunities beyond domestic service or agricultural work. Landowners lacked the cash to maintain the great houses. During both wars, some houses were requisitioned by the government and were left in poor condition, with their owners unable to afford restoration. Nearly 1,000 English country houses were torn down in the decade after the end of the Second World War.

At Chawton, land was sold off, piece by piece (some for as little as £30 an acre), and the Great House was divided into flats. Caroline Knight, born in 1970 and a member of the last generation of Knights to grow up in the Great House, said that she understood from childhood that "the financial burden of the house was unsustainable and the Knight family was not going to be able to continue, practically, to live in Chawton."

Restoration and Reuse

In 1987, Richard Knight, the great-grandnephew of Montagu Knight, inherited Chawton House, which was by then in need of extensive repairs. Searching for a way to save the house from further decline, he leased the house and gardens for a period of 125 years to the Chawton House Library charity, founded by Sandy Lerner and funded by the Leonard X. Bosack and Betty M. Kruger Foundation. Lerner, an American entrepreneur with strong interests in Jane Austen, other English women writers, traditional farming, and equestrian pursuits, restored the house, which opened in 2003 as Chawton House Library. Her rare book collection forms the core of the library, which focuses on works by women writers from 1600 through 1830. The family library collection of the Knights, much of which dates from the 18th and 19th centuries, is on loan from Richard Knight, who serves as a trustee of Chawton

House Library. A collection of modern critical and reference material and the books and research papers of Austen scholar Deirdre Le Faye are also housed in the library.

Today, visiting scholars work in the reading rooms in the Great House and stay in the converted Old Stables. Chawton House Library hosts several academic conferences each year, and the Jane Austen Society of the UK holds its annual meetings on the

Sandy Lerner and Richard Knight with Edward Knight's portrait, which returned to Chawton House in 2010.

grounds. Tourists and students visit the house to see the library, learn about the estate, and visit the room where Jane Austen is said to have sat and contemplated the landscape outside the window.

In 1813, Austen wrote about her brother Edward's plan to create a new kitchen-garden on the rise behind the house. This walled garden has now been restored and is home to edible and ornamental plants. In 1809, carpenter Thomas Jones billed Edward Knight for work on a garden glass-house, a recreation of which is soon to be built. An early barn, moved from a site in Alton, stands in the meadow. Shire horses graze in the fields and haul logs from the woods, just as horses did two centuries ago. Over 7,000 new trees have been planted in the parkland, where diverse wild plants and flowers grow, and tenant farmers' sheep roam the pastures. The historic landscape is being restored and preserved, but it is not just a picture of the past: Chawton House Library is making a positive contribution to the local ecology and educating the public about sustainable land use and conservation.

A shire horse grazes in front of farm buildings at Chawton House.

Chawton Park Wood is now under the control of the UK Forestry Commission and is open for recreational purposes. Using online map applications, one can see wooded areas identified by the names that were already old when Edward Knight came to know them, such as Ackender, Bushy Leaze, and Imbook Copse. Evidence of formerly coppiced trees can still be seen in parts of the parkland around Chawton House.

In the village of Chawton, the cottages are no longer inhabited by farm workers and impoverished widows looking to the Great House for employment or charity. While the village is rightfully proud of its historical assets, the community in which Chawton House Library and Jane Austen's House Museum now participate extends around the world.

Afterword

Many people have tried their hand at writing fiction that intersects with Austen's novels, adding scenes within her stories or projecting the future lives of her characters. Without making any claim to literary merit, I offer the following vignettes simply as illustrations of the challenges and opportunities involved in estate ownership, using some of her characters.

An expansion of a familiar scene at the beginning of Pride and Prejudice:

At Netherfield with Mr. Bingley and his sisters, Mr. Darcy passes the time responding to letters from Pemberley. One of these is from his steward: knowing that Mr. Darcy would approve, given the remarkably high price of wheat, he has given £10 for bread for the poor, and has bought a set of scales for use by the bread-weighers, who are in charge of ensuring that bakers' loaves weigh what they are supposed to.

Mr. Darcy also has a letter from his sister Georgiana, passing on some local gossip: the ten children of Richard Arkwright, the Derbyshire cotton-spinning and banking magnate, came down to breakfast one day and found, tucked into each of their napkins, a £10,000 bank note—the equivalent of Mr. Darcy's income for the year. The Darcy fortune, based on land, has grown in a slow and dignified manner since his own father's day, and, as he looks over at the Bingleys (whose pleasures and aspirations are made possible by their late father's success in trade), Mr. Darcy begins to understand just how significantly the nature of wealth in England is changing.[36]

A scene based on Emma, *set after the novel's close, in 1816*:

Crossing the meadows toward Abbey Mill Farm, Mr. Knightley considers what he is going to say to Robert Martin. The two men have spent many hours together discussing the Corn Law, the strange weather, Knightley's sheep, and Martin's crops. All around them, farmers are distressed: this year's harvest has been the worst in memory,

---

[36] *The donation for bread and purchase of a bread scale are found in the Knight accounts book. Richard Arkwright II did indeed surprise his children on several occasions with such gifts.*

and those who took on debt during the war years are having trouble meeting their commitments. They complain about the number of the unemployed and the constant rise in the parochial rates, even as they cut their laborers' work-days. The farmers' recent appeal to the rector (who lives at a distance from Highbury), asking him to reduce his tithes, has met with an immediate refusal—an unsurprising result, considering that Mr. Elton, the vicar, carried the message.

Robert Martin is struggling, too; only his pride and his wife's prudence have kept him from falling behind on his rent. Knightley is not worried about him, however. Martin is a good manager and a scientific farmer, whose attention to the agricultural reports and demonstrations of new machinery has paid off. In fact, the two men have the opportunity to not just weather the troubled times, but to get ahead. A farm adjacent to the Donwell land is for sale, at a price well below what it would have brought just three years ago. Such a purchase would be a risk—Knightley would have to draw on Emma's money, and he has already spoken with Mr. Cox about a potential mortgage—but if Martin can take on the tenancy and work the two farms as one, both men can benefit.

A scene based on Persuasion, *looking ahead to 1818:*

Sir William Elliot sits in the dim library in Kellynch Hall, glass and bottle at his elbow. Mr. Shepherd, the agent for his estate—who is also his father-in-law—has just left. Sir William cannot understand how his life could be so difficult. It had all looked so easy, during those years when he was waiting for Sir Walter Elliot to die so he could inherit Kellynch. Surely an estate-owner should not have to do anything but ride around his park, shoot his birds, and watch his rents roll in? Yet Mr. Shepherd had just given a highly disquieting report on rents: three farmers had not paid on Michaelmas, and the tenant of one of Sir William's largest properties had simply disappeared. Prospective new tenants are scarce, and the few who have come to see the farms have looked askance at the poorly maintained barns and the hedges in need of mending. Sir William is still paying off the mortgages Sir Walter had taken. He has sold off the estate's timber—which was not as helpful as he had hoped, what with every other landowner doing the same thing and the Navy building no new ships. He doubts that any further effort to retrench will help. Perhaps, he thinks, it is time to think about selling some land.

Appendix: Financial Analysis

Two questions were central to my research: First, what was Edward Knight's income (both gross and net) from his Hampshire properties? And second, what was his total income from all of his property in Hampshire, Kent, and other counties? The first question could be answered with precision, but the second required several sources to be compared and some assumptions to be made. These are described below.

Key Resources

The principal record that sheds light on Edward Knight's business activities in Hampshire is the estate accounts book for 1808 through 1819 (Hampshire Record Office catalog number 79M78/B211). Knight's agents, Robert Trimmer and then Charles Trimmer, summarized each year's activity in a standard format, ready for inspection by Edward Knight. The yearly summaries in the accounts book include the date and amount in which deposits were made to Knight's bank. The accounts book for 1820 through 1832 is missing from the archives, but the next book, beginning in 1833, has survived (HRO 79M78/B212).

A similar accounts book, though formatted differently, exists for the Kent estates for the period 1854 through 1875 (HRO 39M89/B648). A rent book for the Kent property, containing a list of farms, tenants, and rent payments but no details of income from other sources, exists for the period 1848 through 1874 (HRO 39M89/E/B447). A survey, dated 1815, of Knight's property in Kent provides acreage and the names of occupiers, allowing rental property to be distinguished from lands-in-hand, but amounts of rent paid are not included (Godmersham Heritage Centre catalog number SF/G/1/11 2010.777).

Edward Knight's primary London bank was Goslings Bank, which later became part of Barclays. His account ledgers are held by Barclays Group Archives, whose archivist graciously provided copies to me for certain years. Knight's accounts run from 1794 through 1808 under the name Edward Austen, and from March 1816 onward under the Knight surname. Knight apparently suspended his Goslings account and used his brother Henry's firm (initially Austen, Maunde, & Austen, and later Austen, Maunde, & Tilson) as his London bank from 1808 through 1815. If records of Henry's bank survived, their whereabouts are unknown.

Analysis of Earnings and Profits from Hampshire Properties

Determining Edward Knight's income from his Hampshire properties was relatively straightforward. Using each annual summary, I subtracted the amount carried over from a prior year to identify the gross earnings (all money received) for each year:

Gross earnings (excluding money carried over from a prior year)

Year	1808	1809	1810	1811	1812	1813	1814	1815	1816	1817	1818	1819
£	4,310	4,435	5,128	5,276	5,654	5,579	5,259	4,332	4,392	5,341	5,444	7,693

Next, I added together all the expenses for each year:

Expenses

Year	1808	1809	1810	1811	1812	1813	1814	1815	1816	1817	1818	1819
£	1,328	1,349	1,500	1,505	2,061	3,207	2,549	2,074	2,104	2,377	2,645	2,935

Money that was not consumed by expenses represents net income (or net profit):

Net profit

Year	1808	1809	1810	1811	1812	1813	1814	1815	1816	1817	1818	1819
£	2,982	3,086	3,628	3,771	3,593	2,372	2,710	2,258	2,288	2,964	2,799	4,758

Filling in the Gaps

After 1819, assumptions and speculation become necessary. The absence of an estate accounts book for 1820 through 1832 has made it difficult to trace the lingering effects of Knight's 1816-1818 financial difficulties and to examine the impacts of Edward Knight II's permanent residence at Chawton House, beginning in 1826, and the related changes to land use. The Goslings account records provide some insight into this period, however. Deposits of money from the Hampshire properties were sent to Goslings through the banking firm of Stevens & Co. (sometimes written Stephens), located in Farnham, where Knight's agent Charles Trimmer maintained an office. This deposit data is not precisely comparable to the "net profit" figures given above for 1808 through 1819, as the money deposited in the bank was only a portion of Knight's net income (other amounts being taken as cash-in-hand, a practice that increased considerably once Edward Knight II settled in Chawton).

Bank Deposits of Hampshire Income, 1820-1833

Year	1820	1821	1822	1823	1824	1825	1826	1827	1828	1829	1830	1831	1832
£	3,569	3,526	1,300	1,000	2,000	943	2,543	2,364	3,535	3,175	1,646	3,312	2,045

Without additional information, it is impossible to conclusively explain the variations in deposit levels. Low earnings, retention of income to cover debts, or capital investments—or several of these at once—are possible. For example, in 1823, Knight's bank account shows a payment of £6,000 to Francis Penystone, Esq., a man from Oxfordshire who owned property in Chawton. Another source shows that this payment is for purchase of a farm called Wood Barn in Chawton; some of the Hampshire income may have been retained to apply toward it. (The earlier Hampshire accounts book does contain examples of land purchase money being paid out by Knight's agent.) Then again, other factors may also have been at work, as Knight's account was unusually active in that year, with over £7,000 of stock sold, what appears to be £3,000 raised by mortgaging property, and deposits totaling £1,639 from Levy & Co. (This firm had originated as Baverstock & Levy, a bank in Alton in which one of the partners was Knight's former legal opponent, James Baverstock. Levy lost Baverstock as a partner after the latter's bankruptcy and acquired Charles Trimmer, Edward Knight's agent.) Levy & Co. had also made deposits totaling £839 in 1822. I believe these deposits to be loans or possibly mortgage proceeds, because in 1823 Knight began to make payments back to Levy & Co., usually £100 at a time, totaling £930 in that year.

Knight's Hampshire estate income deposits hit a new low in 1825, and he received another (presumed) loan from Levy & Co., this time for £1,000. Knight's financial position had already been weakened by the preceding bad years, and his efforts to sell his London property, to sell dwelling-houses in Alton, and to find a new tenant for Chawton Great House, all in 1825, suggest the impact of the continuing economic depression.[37] Nonetheless, Knight continued to repay Levy & Co. steadily, paying £1,200 in 1825.

Looking Beyond Hampshire: Income from Other Properties

Income from the Hampshire properties was just a part of Edward Knight's financial picture. To determine the rest, I analyzed deposits to his Goslings bank account, looking for a pattern of deposits that would suggest Knight's agents in other counties regularly forwarding rents and proceeds from other estate business. Notations in the records of the country banks that submitted the deposits made it possible to identify the properties where particular income streams originated.

---

[37] *Neither the contemplated Great House rental or the sale of May's Buildings were completed at this time. An advertisement for the Alton buildings appears in the* Hampshire Chronicle.

Hammond & Co., located in Canterbury, consistently made large deposits. These deposits represent the proceeds of Kent estate business.

Other routine deposits stand out. An individual named Hugh Russell regularly deposited money directly to Knight's account, without sending it through an intermediary bank, between 1816 and 1825. In 1826, a Mr. Morgan seems to have taken over. I believe Russell and Morgan were Knight's agents in charge of the rental properties called May's Buildings on St. Martin's Lane, London. A ratebook, circa 1800, shows a Hugh Russell living at 44 St. Martin's Lane.

Over the entire 1816-1833 period for which I examined Knight's Goslings Bank records, deposits were made from Sparrow & Co., an Essex bank. Some of those entries include the name Thomas Blyth, Esq.—most likely a long-term tenant of a single, large Knight-owned property in that area. A man by that name farmed at a property called Highfield in Langham, Essex, during the period in question; while I have not been able to connect him conclusively to Knight, he is a good candidate to be the tenant whose rent payments were forwarded through Sparrow & Co. to Goslings Bank.

The money flow for Knight's Sussex property is unclear. Knight's Hampshire agent Charles Trimmer recorded combined deposits of Hampshire and Sussex moneys sent to Goslings on three occasions, once in 1816 (in which the Sussex portion was £349) and twice in 1817 (£493 and £497). The approximate annual rent of the Sussex property, £990, can be estimated from this data (bearing in mind that variations in rent payments frequently occurred due to reimbursement for repairs, taxes, and the like). Perhaps in other years Sussex payments were forwarded to Knight directly, or were bundled with other deposits without annotation.

Consolidated Financial Picture

Bank deposits related to Knight's estate business, consolidated by year across all sources, are shown below.

Year	1817	1818	1819	1820	1821	1822	1823
£	5,496	10,348	3,685	4,779	4,780	2,977	8,648

Year	1824	1825	1826	1827	1828	1829	1830
£	7,266	2,889	3,232	3,594	4,865	4,503	2,525

Again, caveats apply. Not all estate income was put in the bank, and not all money put in the bank was estate income. Some of the deposits represent debt. In 1818, for example, deposits from Hammond & Co., Knight's Canterbury bank, were more than triple the previous year's deposits. A logical deduction is that Knight obtained a loan from Hammond & Co. to meet his expenses in settling the Baverstock lawsuit, but exactly what proportion of the Hammond deposits represent such a loan is unknown. Other years in which loans are probable, based on the frequency and amount of Hammond & Co. deposits, are 1824 and 1825.

Overall, the Hammond & Co. deposits, which average £500 per year in the years when no suspected loan deposits are present, are too low to represent Knight's total earnings from his Kent holdings. It is assumed that he would have taken a portion of his Kent income as cash-in-hand to meet day-to-day expenses rather than sending it to the bank. In 1815, when a survey of Knight's property in Kent was performed, he owned 2,400 acres there, about one-third of the amount he owned in Hampshire. He had less woodland in Kent, but actively farmed his lands-in-hand. As in Hampshire, rental income would have been a key component of revenue. In Kent, Knight owned 874 acres of land rented to tenants. In 1848, the earliest year for which I have been able to make a like-to-like comparison of rental income, Knight's Hampshire rents totaled £3,943, Kent rents £3,610—but changes to the holdings in each county had occurred since 1815, including the purchase of over 1,000 acres in Molash, Kent, between 1816 and 1847.

In trying to develop a comparative picture of Knight's rental income, I have focused on the year 1817, the year for which the most data sources are available and uncertainties and ambiguities are the fewest. For that year, rental income is known for Hampshire and Sussex (from the estate accounts book), and for London and Essex (from the Goslings ledgers, if my assumption is correct that income from those locations is purely rent).

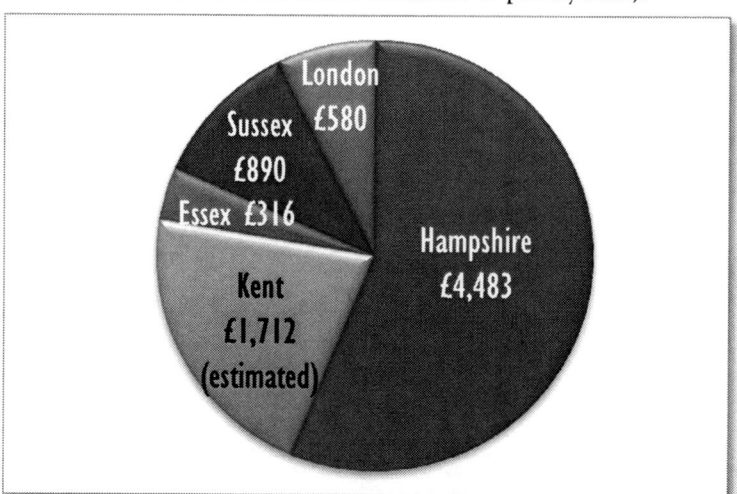

Sources of Edward Knight's rental income for 1817.

Only the rental income for Kent is unknown. Assuming that the Molash farms purchased before 1817 added about 500 acres, and using a land rental rate of £1.5.0 an acre,[38] an estimated total rental value for the Kent lands in 1817 is £1,712. This would yield an estimated total rental income for 1817 of £7,981.

Despite the large uncertainties inherent in this analysis, one fact is clear: during the early 19th century, Edward Knight's Hampshire properties were, year in and year out, the source of about half of his total income, and were essential to his ability to maintain the life he and his family enjoyed and to preserve his estates for the next generation.

Limitations in Research

The ability to examine Edward Knight's day-to-day banking activity and to compare it to other sources of information about his activities opens up many possible avenues of study. Having focused primarily on Knight's business in Hampshire during the period when Jane Austen resided in Chawton, and having pursued his banking records to answer a few basic questions, I have not studied other aspects of those records in great detail. Nor has it been possible to compare the bank records to the full body of deeds and other property records in the Knight Archive and in the collections of the Godmersham Heritage Centre. Bank ledgers prior to Knight's transfer of his account to Austen, Maunde, & Austen also await full examination. Such research could provide a more detailed picture of Knight's activities in Kent and his property holdings over time.

---

[38] *Writing for the Board of Agriculture, Arthur Young determined this figure in 1813 as an average rental price for "excellent arable land" on the foot of the South Downs in Sussex; this is roughly comparable, geographically and chronologically. This £1.5.0 per acre figure may be overly generous, however. Knight charged £0.16.0 per acre for two of his Chawton farms during the same general period.*

References and Bibliography

This book leans heavily on two sources in the Hampshire Record Office: the estate accounts book (79M78/B211) that Robert Trimmer began in 1808, when he assumed the role of Edward Knight's agent after the death of Bridger Seward, as well as bundles of pay vouchers, bills, and receipts (39M89/E/B705, 39M89/E/B312, and 39M89/E/B314) that substantiate the expenses summarized in the accounts book. **Statements in the text of Knight's yearly finances and information on specific payments and income, if not otherwise attributed, are based on these sources, which are not included in the reference table that appears in this section.** Calculations and other analyses of the financial figures contained in these sources are the author's work. Any researcher requiring more specific information on sources is welcome to contact the author at linda@woodpigeonpublishing.com.

Goslings Bank Ledgers held by Barclays Group Archives are numbered as follows:

1805	130.43-81	1820	130.203-45	1826	130.226-413
1806	130.43-82		130.203-46		130.226-414
1807	130.43-82		130.203-47		130.226-415
	130.151-75		130.203-48		130.226-416
1808	130.151-75	1821	130.203-124	1827	130.226-416
1816	130.187-105		130.211-42		130.226-417
	130.187-470		130.211-43		130.234-482
	130.187-471		130.211-48		130.234-483
1817	130.187-471		130.211-49	1828	130.234-484
	130.187-482	1822	130.211-43		130.234-485
	130.187-452		130.211-44	1829	130.234-486
	130.195-47	1823	130.219-26		130.234-489
	130.195-48		130.219-27	1830	130.242-490
1818	130.195-48		130.211-45		130.242-491
	130.195-49		130.211-46		130.242-492
	130.195-50	1824	130.219-27	1831	130.242-492
	130.195-51		130.219-28		130.242-493
1819	130.195-52		130.219-29		130.250-527
	130.195-53		130.219-30	1832	130.250-528
	130.203-44	1825	130.219-452		130.250-529
	130.203-45		130.219-453	1833	130.250-529
			130.226-412		130.250-530
			130.226-413		
			130.219-30		

The table that follows provides reference information for specific topics (given in shortened form in italics) that appear on the pages indicated. All dates are given in American format, MM/DD/YYYY. For a cited author with multiple works in the bibliography, a title keyword follows the author's name to indicate which work is intended.

Abbreviations as used in the table of references are:

GHC   Godmersham Heritage Centre
HC   *Hampshire Chronicle*
HRO   Hampshire Record Office
HT   *Hampshire Telegraph*
KG   *Kentish Gazette*
L   *Jane Austen's Letters*, letter number cited as in 4th edition
S&WJ   *Salisbury and Winchester Journal*
TNA   The National Archives

Page	References
Ack'ts	*American:* 1M70/PO3
1	*1820 letter:* Austen-Leigh, R.A. *Gipsies:* HRO 79M78/b211.
3	*Steventon villager:* L13, 12/1-2/1798.
7	*General biography:* Le Faye, Record; Sutherland. *Grand Tour Journal:* Spence.
8	*Legal proceedings:* Sutherland. *Deputy lieutenant and military service:* Caplan, Volunteers. *Magistrate:* KG 6/30/1812. *High sheriff:* Ancestor. *Hospital:* HRO 18M61/Box D/Bundle 7/Part 1.
9	*Societies:* KG 5/26/1835. *Collections:* KG 6/81847, HC 11/4/1822, HC 3/27/1815; Morning Post, 5/18/1822. *Ireland:* KG 12/15/1835. *Anna Lefroy:* Le Faye, Record. *Cassandra letter:* Wilson. *Fanny's cow:* Wilson. *Touring with son:* Hillan. *Man of Business:* Le Faye, Reminiscences. *Canals:* HC 12/21/1807. *Railways:* KG 3/14/1837. *Market:* KG 3/12/1833. *Blossoms:* Le Faye, Record. *Happiness:* L15 12/24-26/1798.
10	*Hairstyle:* L18 1/21-23/1799. *Sunshine:* L98 3/5-8/1814. *Complaints:* L15 12/24-26/1798. *Bustle:* L19 5/17/1799. *Electricity:* L20 6/2/1799. *Party:* L71, 4/25/1811. *King:* L102, 6/23/1814. *Dentist:* L87, 9/15-16/1813. *Misses:* London Standard, 12/21/1827. *Paris:* LeFaye, Fanny Knight's Diaries. *Europe:* Chronology. *Marquess:* Bennet. *Ledgers:* Goslings.
11	*Income:* L17 9/8-9/1799. *Elegance:* L55, 6/30/1808. *Economy:* L55 6/30-7/1/1808. *1820 letter:* Austen-Leigh, R.A. *Trustees:* TNA PROB 11/2163/310. *Henhouse, pigs:* L15 12/24-26/1798. *Renovations:* L91, 10/11-12, 1813. *Memorandums:* L101, 6/14/1814.
12	*1824:* HRO 39M89/F111/5. *1824 letter:* HRO 39M89/F11/5/1-2. *George:* HRO 18M61/Box D/Bundle 7/Part 1; HRO 39M89/E/B314/1-14; Hurst, Poor George Austen? *Henry:* Bennet. *Lawyers:* HRO 39M89/E/T140. *Annuities:* HRO 18M61/Box 84/Misc16/Item 1. *Marianne:* Hillan. *Obituary:* Gentleman's Magazine. *Will:* TNA Prob 11/2163. *Tenantry:* KG - Tuesday 30 November 1852.
13	*Brodnax history:* Austen-Leigh & Knight; Le Faye, Chronology; Dunning.
15	*Broke entail:* Corley. *Ford Place:* Le Faye, Jane Austen's Country Life. *Godmersham acreage:* GHC SF/G/1/11 2010.777. *Gentleman's seat, sportsmen:* Bannister. *Serpentine walk, river walk:* Le Faye, Country Life. *Improvements:* Austen-Leigh, R.A. *1774 list:* 39M89/E/B114&115. *Hampshire acreage:* Vancouver. *55 manors, descent of estate:* Austen-Leigh & Knight. *Royal road:* Duthy.
16	*Steventon transformation:* Morrin. *Chawton enclosure:* HRO 39M89/E/B449. *Enclosure:* Hammond & Hammond.
17	*Oxfordshire, Devon:* HRO Knight Archive index. *Sussex, Essex. Middlesex:* See Appendix. *1815 estate inheritance document:* HRO 17M28/143.

Page	References
19	*Statements of income as rent:* Smollett; Gloucester Freeholder.
21	*Heron:* HRO 18M61/Box D/Bundle 7/Part 2. *Grain prices:* HC 4/28/1800. *Poor rates:* Ernle. *Year without summer:* Le Faye, Country Life.
22	*Bank failure:* Ellis; Caplan, Banker. *War Office:* Le Faye, Chronology. *Legal expenses:* HRO 39M89/E/T140. *Bank deposits, stock sale, exchequer bills:* Goslings.
23	*1818 estimates:* Corley. *Family expenses:* Goslings ledgers.
24	*Austen on Catherine Knight:* L17 1/8/1799. *1824 letter:* HRO 39M89/F11/5/1-2. *Bank loan:* HRO 39M89/F119/2.
26	*Independence:* Ellis.
27	*Hop growing:* Mudie. *Rent changes:* HRO 39M89/E/B252. *Lease terms:* HRO 39M89/E/B11; HRO 39M89/E/B252.
28	*Cutting trees:* HRO 39M89/E/B641/1-13. *Baigen:* HC 12/7/1801. *Shared costs:* HRO 39M89/B/B252. *Woolveridge:* HRO 39M89/EB384/19.
29	*15% return:* HC 7/23/1821. *Letter to agent:* HRO 39M89/E/B568/15. *Robert Hall:* HRO 39M89/E/B238/1/22, 39M89/E/B238/4. *Mrs. Hall:* Le Faye, Chronology. *Audit:* HRO 39M89/E/B705.
30	*Godmersham rent day:* L86 7/3-6/1813. *Tilson:* L75 6/6/1811. *Navy ships:* Quarterly Review. *Sales of wood:* KG 7/10/1812, HC 6/27/1814, *Beech wood book:* HRO 39M89/E/B642. *Plan of cuts:* HRO 39M89/E, B264(1), HRO 39M89/E/B641/1-13. *Planning:* HRO 39M89/E/B641/12.
31	*900 acres, products:* HRO 39M89/E/B642.
32	*Swathe:* Le Faye, Reminiscences. *Advertisement:* HC 2/08/1819.
33	*Woods notice:* HC 9/28/1801. *Pigs:* KG 9/20/1808, KG 9/231808, KG 10/14/1808, KG 10/18/1808, S&WJ, 8/8/1808.
34	*Game Laws:* Kelly, H. *Gleaning:* Hammond & Hammond. *Theft of wood:* HC 1/21/1793, HC 10/13/1800, HC 5/3/1824, HC 6/22/1807, HC 3/25/1811, HC 9/20/1810, HC 4/7/1823, HC 7/16/1821. *Manorial system:* Flood and Futers. *Manors:* HRO 25M99/25/1.
36	*Quit rents collected:* HRO 79M78/B219.
37	*Land tax:* Pearsall; Ernle; HRO Q22/1/1/8. *Redeeming land tax:* HRO 39M89/E/B727. *Property tax:* GB Customs.
38	*Church rates:* HRO 1M70/PW1. *Two pence:* HRO 39M89/E/B312/1-8.
39	*Hinton tithes:* 39M89/E/B545/2.
40	*Insurance:* HRO 39M89/E/B312/2/8; 39M89/E/B705; HRO 18M61/Tin Box C/Bundle 7. *Livestock insurance:* Devizes and Wiltshire Gazette, 11/1/1855.
41	*Commission, tithe, transport, sales:* HRO 39M89/E/B642. *Agricultural wages:* Royal Society; Young.
42	*Harwoods:* Le Faye, Reminiscences. *Land exchange:* HRO 18M61/Box 84/Misc 16/Item 1.
43	*Winchester:* Grover. *Mortgages, Molash, Pontus:* HRO 39M89/E/T140. *Randall:* HRO 39M89/E/B641/2.
44	*Doctor:* HRO 39M89/E/B705. *Cottages let to parish:* HRO 39M89/PL2&3. *1788 responses:* HRO 21M65/B4/3/30/1. *1819 Survey:* House of Commons, 1819. *Stacey:* HRO 21M65/B4/3/30/1.
45	*U.S. giving:* Forbes.

Page	References
46	*Smith collection:* HT, 8/5 1822, HC 9/2/1822, HC 11/4/1822, Oxford Journal, 2/7/1824. *Colquhoun on poverty:* Colquhoun.
47	*Seating plans:* HRO 39M89/R31/1-2. *John White:* Austen.
48	*1811 survey:* House of Commons, 1812.
50	*Railings:* HRO 39M89/E/B616. *Kentish Papillons:* L145 9/8-9/1816.
51	*Advertisement:* HRO 39M89/H21.
52	*Middleton moves, meetings, remembrances:* Le Faye research notebook, CHL. *Other houses:* HRO 31M71/T6; HRO 27A01/B1/3/10; S&WJ, 3/7/1803. *Maria and Lucy:* HRO 23M93/84/1-4. *Browning:* HRO 39M89/E/B705.
53	*Bailiff salary:* GB Board of Agriculture, Hampshire. *John Heath:* HRO 39M89/E/B252. *Robert Trimmer as lawyer:* HC 12/22/1800, HC 8/12/1805.
54	*C. Trimmer in law, bank, insurance:* HC 6/7/1813, HC 9/25/1815, HC 8/26/1822, HC 11/20/1826.
55	*Heath's job:* HRO 39M89/E/B682. *Randall benefits:* HRO 39M89/E/B516/2.
56	*Steward's office:* Carpenter, Tom, personal communication. *Seward will:* TNA Prob 11/1478. *Association:* HC 4/24/1786. *Sheep fair:* HC 8/12/1797. *Canal meeting:* HC 12/21/1807.
57	*Pianoforte:* Wilson.
58	*19 servants:* Austen-Leigh, R.A. *Cassandra's tapes:* L89 9/23-24/1813; Rees & Rees.
59	*Turner:* L1016/14/1814. *Pullinger salary:* HRO 39M89/H21. *Cucumbers:* HC 3/27/1826; HC 3/24/1828; HC 3/30/1829. *Garden:* HRO 39M89/H20.
60	*House pulled down:* HRO 18M61/Box 84/Misc 16/Item 1. *Salary:* HRO 39M89/H21.
61	*JA letters on Triggs:* L155 3/23-25/1817; L88 9/16/1813; L102 6/23/1814. *Ann & Jane Triggs:* Hurst, Jane, personal communication. *George Triggs:* HT, 9/14/1835; Willet. *Walter Triggs:* Hampshire Advertiser, 3/18/1871. *William Triggs:* HC9/11/1826, S&WJ, 12/10/1832.
63	*Sussex Agricultural Society:* Sussex Advertiser, 11/1/1813.
64	*Chawton, Farringdon women:* Wages book, 1907-1912, Chawton House Library. *Rout, Ewens, Smith:* HC 6/28/1802. *Garnett:* HC, 11/8/1819. *Churchwardens:* HRO 1M70/PW1.
65	*Showing timber:* HC 3/13/1826, HC 11/22/1830. *Rent:* HRO 79M78/B212. *Overseers:* 1M70/PO3. *Tower captain:* Parry, Sarah, personal communication. *Headstone:* Pearson.
66	*Overseers:* 1M70/PO3. *Park View Cottages:* Hurst, JA and Chawton. *Allotments:* KG 11/19/1833.
67	*Stabbing:* Le Faye, Notes & Queries; S&WJ, 3/14/1814. *Lived to 80:* Knight, T & L; Hurst personal communication. *Elizabeth Mersh:* 1M70/PO3. *Baby:* HRO 21M65/F8/50/1. *HAC premium:* HC 11/11/1876. *1790 assessment:* Selwyn.
68	*9-1/2 miles:* HRO 21M65/B4/3/30/1, HRO 1M70/PV1. *Asylum:* HC 12/26/1814.
69	*Odiham society:* Le Faye, Country Life. *Hampshire Agricultural Society:* HT, 9/16/1811.
70	*Consolidation:* HC 22nd Feb 1802.
71	*Woolveridge:* HC 2/3/1817, HC 3/17/1817. *1827 tenants:* HRO 39M89/E/B568/11. *Fire insurance:* HRO 18M61/Tin Box C/Bundle 7.

Page	References
72	*Dinner in barn:* Le Faye (ed.), Reminiscences. *James Austen's table:* Le Faye, Chronology. *George Austen:* Hurst, Poor George Austen; HRO 39M89/E/B/314/1-14. *Alton House:* HC 6/10/1811. *Grecian sofa, chairs, pony chaise:* HC 5/27/1822.
73	*Terry legacy:* documented April 1813, Hurst pers. comm. *Turnip seeds:* Reading Mercury, 5/18/1801. *Threshing machine:* Royal Society. *Sheep and cows:* HC 5/27/1822. *Earl of St. Vincent:* HT, 5/27/1805. *SPCK:* HT, 9/13 1813. *Provident Savings Bank:* HC 1/25/1819. *Agricultural Society:* HT, 9/16/1811, HC 6/19/1820, HC 6/18/1821. HC 11/8/1819. *Brussels:* Dalrymple; HRO 44M69/F10/65/2. *Auction:* HC 5/27/1822.
74	*Harry's death:* Salisbury and Winchester Journal, 4/1/1848. *William's death:* Le Faye, Chronology. *Andrews biography:* Hurst, Poor Farmer Andrews; Hurst, personal communication. *New Park Farm crops:* 39M89/E/B563/8.
75	*Deputation:* HC 9/17/1804. *Fanny Knight diary:* Le Faye, Fanny Knight. *1815 letter:* L128 11/26/1815. *Woolls interaction:* L142 7/9/1816.
76	*Dyers' business and house:* Hurst, JA and Alton; Hurst, personal communication.
78	*Golds' house:* Hurst, Chawton. *Land tax:* HRO Q22/1/1/8.
79	*Overseers:* 1M70/PO3. *Starving paupers:* HC 3/31/1823. *Gold will:* March 1836, microfiche at HRO.
81	*David Papillon:* KG 6/9/1809; Bentley. *Henry Austen's offer:* JAS Cambridge.
82	*Fanny Knight:* Le Faye, Chronology. *Rectory property:* 1798 Chawton terrier, HRO. *Lexden:* Cooper and Elrington. *Curate:* Ellis. *Tithe reduction:* Salisbury and Winchester Journal 12/18/1815. *St. Thomas's Day:* Hurst, Christmas. SPCK: HT 9/13/1813. *Germany:* HC 4/7/1814. *Female asylum:* HC 6/30/1817. *Peterloo:* HC 10/11/1819, 10/25/1819. *Selborne parson:* HC 1/20/1823.
83	*School:* Cooper & Elrington.
84	*House search:* L53 6/20-22/1808, L56 10/1-2/1808. *Remarkably pretty:* L62 12/9/1808.
85	*Book society:* Le Faye, Letters, p589. *Clinker's shop:* L102 6/23/1814. *Dilapidated tenements:* Hampshire Archives. *John White:* Austen. *Walked to Gt. House:* L101 6/14/1814.
86	*Harriet Knight:* L148 1/8/1817. *Garnetts:* L78 1/24/1813. *Observer:* Austen. *High walls:* Sutherland. *Locked back gate:* L80 2/4/1813.
87	*Edward II as child:* L60 10/24-25/1808.
88	*As young man:* L90 9/25/1813. *Winchester and Oxford:* Whitstable Times 11/15/1879. *Meetings on case:* HRO 39M89/E/T140. *Turned 21:* Wilson. *Allowance:* Goslings ledgers. *"Ever the first":* Baily. *Cricket:* HC 8/9/1824. *1820 Parliament:* S&WJ 3/6/1820. *EHAC founding:* Hampshire Advertiser, 12th Mar 1842. *Deputy lieutenant:* Whitstable Times 11/15/1879. *Sheriff:* HRO 39M89/H11/1-29, HC 7/7/1823. *Races steward:* HC 8/4/1823.
89	*Parliament, Rochester:* History of Parliament. *Elopement:* Hillan. *"Lucky fellow":* HRO 23M93/62/2/9. *Vestry:* HRO 1M70/PV1. *Magistrate, senior magistrate:* Whitstable Times 11/15/1879. *Church repairs:* S&WJ 5/29/1837. *Friendly Society:* Hants Advertiser 7/13/1867. *EHAC:* Reading Mercury 11/8/1856. *Rifle corps:* HT 11/5/1864. *Mechanics Institute:* Reading Mercury 6/3/1854. *Livestock insurance:* Devizes and Wiltshire Gazette 11/1/1855.
90	*Master of hunt:* Whitstable Times 11/15/1879. *Festivities:* KG 1/30/1849, Hampshire Advertiser, 7/27/1872. *New Domesday:* Reading Mercury, 4/22/1876.

Page	References
91	*Shalden, Wivelrod:* HRO 17M48/162. *Steventon:* HRO 39M89/E/B75. *Godmersham:* Austen-Leigh & Knight. *All but two properties:* Knight, Jeremy, personal communication; Austen-Leigh & Knight. *Sheep:* HRO 79M78/B212. *1907 wages book:* Chawton House Library. *Elizabeth Knight:* HRO 39M89/E/B682.
92	*Challenges for landowners:* Kelly, M.; Parry, Pemberley. *Chawton land sale:* HRO 3M89/E/B41. *Caroline Knight:* Morris. *Chawton House Library:* Parry, Teachers; CHL website.
93	*Kitchen-garden:* L86 7/6/1813. *Landscape improvements:* CHL website.
95	*Richard Arkwright gifts:* Fitton.
98	*Identification of banks here and following:* GB Post Office; Curtis; Hurst, History of Alton.
99	*Wood Barn purchase:* 18M61/Box84/Misc 16/Item. *Baverstock & Levy:* Hurst, History of Alton. *Houses in Alton:* HC 7/18/1825.
100	*London ratebook:* Gater and Hiorns. *Thomas Blyth:* History House.
101	*1815 Kent survey:* Godmersham Heritage Centre. *1848 Hampshire rents:* 79M78/B213. *1848 Kent rents:* 39M89/E/B447.
102	*Arthur Young rental figure:* GB Agriculture, Sussex.

"Aesop." Sporting Reminiscences of Hampshire, 1864.

The Ancestor, A Quarterly Review of County & Family History (periodical), Jan. 1903.

Austen, Caroline. My Aunt Jane Austen, 1991.

Austen-Leigh, R.A. (ed.). Austen Papers, 1704-1856, 1942.

Austen-Leigh, W. and Knight, Montagu G. Chawton Manor and its Owners, 1911.

Baily, A.H. Baily's Magazine of Sports and Pastimes, 1874.

Bannister, Nicola. Godmersham Park Volume 1: Historical Landscape Suevey, Kent Counrt Council, 1995.

Bennet, Stuart. "Lord Moira and the Austens," in Persuasions 35 (Jane Austen Society of North America), 2014.

Bently, Samuel. Literary Anecdotes of the Eighteenth Century, 1812.

Bowyer, T.H. "Middleton, Nathaniel (1750–1807)," Oxford Dictionary of National Biography, 2004.

Caplan, Clive. "Jane Austen, the Volunteers, and the Defense of the Realm," Report of the Jane Austen Society, 2010.

Caplan, Clive. "Jane Austen's Banker Brother: Henry Thomas Austen of Austen & Co.," JASNA Persuasions 20.

Colquhoun, Patrick. Treatise on Indigence, 1806.

Cooper, Janet, and Elrington, C.R. (eds.). "A History of the County of Essex: Volume 9: The Borough of Colchester," Victoria County History.

Corley, T.A.B. "The Austen Family, the Grays, and the Baverstocks," Report of the Jane Austen Society, 2010.

Craik, George. The Pictorial History of England: Being a History of the People: As Well as a History of the Kingdom, 1843.

Craig, Sheryl. Above Vulgar Economy: Jane Austen and Money. Thesis online at kuscholarworks.ku.edu.

Crook, J.M. "Saving England's Heritage," Times Literary Supplement, June 20, 2012.

Curtis, William. A Short History and Description of the Town of Alton in the County of Southampton, 1896.

Dalrymple, Wemyss. *The Economist's New Brussels Guide, Containing a Short Account of Antwerp,*1839

Dunning, Ronald. Genealogy information at Ronald Dunning Family Tree at http://wc.rootsweb.ancestry.com/cgi-bin/igm.cgi?op=GET&db= ronalddunning&id=I1787.

Duthy, J. *Sketches of Hampshire: Embracing the Antiquities, Topography, Etc. of Country Adjacent to the River Itchen,* 1839.

Ellis, Markman. "Jane Austen and the Credit Crunch of 1816," Report of the Jane Austen Society, 2011.

Ernle (Lord). *English Farming: Past and Present,* 1912.

Fitton, R.S. *The Arkwrights: Spinners of Fortune,*1989.

Flood, Sue, and Futers, Carol. "The End of the Manorial System," www.hertsmemories.org.uk.

Forbes.com. "America's Most Generous Companies," 7/16/2013.

Gater, G.H., and Hiorns, F.R. *Survey of London: volume 20: St Martin-in-the-Fields, pt III: Trafalgar Square & Neighbourhood* at British History Online, http://www.british-history.ac.uk/source.aspx?pubid=751.

Gentleman's Magazine, "Edward Knight, Esq." Volume XXXIX, February 1853.

Gloucester Freeholder. *An Address to the Electors of the United Kingdom,* 1818.

Godmersham Heritage Centre. Parish of Godmersham Property Survey, 1815. SF/G/1/11 2010.777

Great Britain, Board of Agriculture. *Agricultural Surveys: Hampshire,* 1813.

Great Britain, Board of Agriculture. *Agricultural Surveys: Sussex,* 1813.

Great Britain, House of Commons. *Abstract of Answers and Returns Made Pursuant to an Act Passed in the 51ˢᵗ Year of His Majesty King George III,* 1812.

Great Britain, House of Commons, *A Digest of Parochial Returns Made in Response to the Select Committee Appointed to Inquire into the Education of the Poor,* 1819.

Great Britain, Parliament. *Appendix to the India Courier Extraordinary: Proceedings of Parliament Relating to W. Hastings,* Volume 6, 1786.

Great Britain, Post Office. *The Post-Office Annual Directory,* 1814.

Great Britain, Revenue and Customs. "A Tax to Beat Napoleon," online at http://webarchive.nationalarchives.gov.uk/+/http://www.hmrc.gov.uk/history/taxhis 1.htm.

Grover, Christine. "Edward Knight's Inheritance: The Chawton, Godmersham, and Winchester Estates," *Persuasions* 35 (JASNA), 2013.

Hammond, J.L. & Barbara. *The Skilled Labourer 1760-1832: A Study in the Government of England before the Reform Bill,* 1920.

Hammond, J.L. & Barbara. *The Village Labourer 1760-1832,* 1970.

Hampshire Archives and Local Studies. Chawton Tithe Map, 1838, online at http://calm.hants.gov.uk.

Hillan, Sophia. *May, Lou, and Cass: Jane Austen's Nieces in Ireland,* 2011.

History House. "History of Langham," online at www.historyhouse.co.uk/placeL/essexl07b.html.

History of Parliament Trust. *History of Parliament Online, 1820-1832, Constituencies, Rochester.*

Hurst, Jane. *A History of Alton, 1800-1850,* 2008.

Hurst, Jane. *Jane Austen and Alton: A Walk Around Jane Austen's Alton,* 2011.

Hurst, Jane. *Jane Austen and Chawton: A Walk Around Jane Austen's Chawton,* 2009.

Hurst, Jane. "Chawton's Christmas Customs," Report of the Jane Austen Society, 2013.

Hurst, Jane. "Poor Farmer Andrews," Report of the Jane Austen Society, 2009.

Hurst, Jane. "Poor George Austen," Report of the Jane Austen Society, 2004.

Jane Austen Society. "Jane Austen and Cambridge," www.janeaustensoci.freeuk.com/pages/branches/cambridge_connections.htm.

Johnson, Paul. *Birth of the Modern: World Society 1815-1830*, 1991.

Kelly, Helena. "Mansfield Park Reconsidered: Pheasants, Game Laws, and the Hidden Critique of Slavery," in *Persuasions* 30 (JASNA), 2008.

Kelly, Mike. "Vanished Inheritances," the Journal, February 20, 2012.

Knight, Tony and Linda. "Chawton Burials," online at http://www.knightroots.co.uk/transcriptions/Parishes_C/Chawton/Burials/burials.htm

Le Faye, Deirdre. *A Chronology of Jane Austen and Her Family*, 2006.

Le Faye, Deirdre. Austen-Leigh, W., Austen-Leigh, R.A. *Jane Austen: A Family Record*, 1989.

Le Faye, Deirdre. *Fanny Knight's Diaries: Jane Austen Through her Niece's Eyes*, 2000.

Le Faye, Deirdre. *Jane Austen's Country Life*, 2014.

Le Faye, Deirdre (ed.). *Reminiscences of Caroline Austen*, Jane Austen Society, 1986.

Le Faye, Deirdre. *Jane Austen's Letters*, 4th edition, 2011.

Milmo, Cahal. "Calls to Abolish Outdated Rights for Lords of the Manor that Serve No Purpose in the 21st Century," The Independent, January 16, 2014.

Morrin, Jean. "Social History and Economic History of Steventon," online at www.victoriacountyhistory.ac.uk/counties/hampshire/work-in-progress/steventon

Morris, Linda. "Jane Austen Descendant Caroline Knight Comes to Grips with her History," Sydney Morning Herald, April 5, 2014.

Mudie, Robert. *Hampshire: Its Past and Present Condition, and Future Prospects*, 1838.

Muir, Richard. *The English Village*, 1980.

Parry, Sarah. "Teacher's Pack for Chawton House Estate," 2012.

Parry, Sarah. "The Pemberley Effect: Austen's Legacy to the Historic House Industry," in Persuasions 30.

Parker, Rowland. *The Common Stream: Two Thousand Years of the English Village*, 1994.

Pearsall, Mark. "The Land Tax 1692-1963," Magazine of the Friends of The National Archives, Vol. 22 No.3, 2011.

Pearson, Mark. "Inscriptions in Chawton Churchyard," online at www.chawton.info, 2001.

Quarterly Review. "On India-Built Ships and Naval Timber," October 1813, January 1814.

Rees, Jane & Rees, Mark. *The Rule Book: Measuring for the Trades*, 2010.

Rotherham, Ian. *Ancient Woodland: History, Industry and Crafts*, 2013.

Royal Society of Arts. *The Complete Farmer: or, a General Dictionary of Husbandry*, 1807.

Selwyn, David. "Making a Living," in *Cambridge Companion to Jane Austen*, 1997.

Smollett, Tobias. *The Critical Review: Or, Annals of Literature*, Volume 36, 1802.

Spence, Jon (ed). *Jane Austen's Brother Abroad*, 2005.

Sutherland, Kathryn (ed.), Austen-Leigh, J.E. *A Memoir of Jane Austen and Other Family Recollections*, 2002.

White, William. *History, Gazetteer and Directory of the County of Hampshire*, 1878.

Willets, Jen. "Free Settler or Felon?," online at http://www.jenwilletts.com/convict_ship_captain_cook_1833.htm

Wilson, Margaret. *Almost Another Sister*, 1990.

Vancouver, Charles. *General View of the Agriculture of Hampshire and the Isle of Wight*, 1810.

Young, Arthur. *Annals of Agriculture, and Other Useful Arts*, 1801.

Linda Slothouber is a Life Member of the Jane Austen Society of North America. Following a career at a leading management and technology consulting firm, she has written for several magazines and journals, contributing articles on antiques, architectural and industrial heritage, and Jane Austen. She holds a Bachelor's degree in Comparative Literature from the University of Virginia and a Master's degree in Administration from the University of Maryland University College.